the science of...

THE
ULTIMATE SURVIVAL GUIDE

Mike Flynn is a former curator in the Education Department at the Science Museum in London and has published widely in the fields of science, technology and mathematics.

A keen fell runner, hiker and a former 400-metre champion, he was recently the martial-arts consultant for a book on vampire slaying.

The Science of . . . brings popular science to a global audience through science-based blockbuster exhibitions and initiatives in other media.

Look out for other **The Science of . . .** books and products in your local stores.

 ASKING THE BIG QUESTIONS ABOUT THE WORLD WE LIVE IN

THE

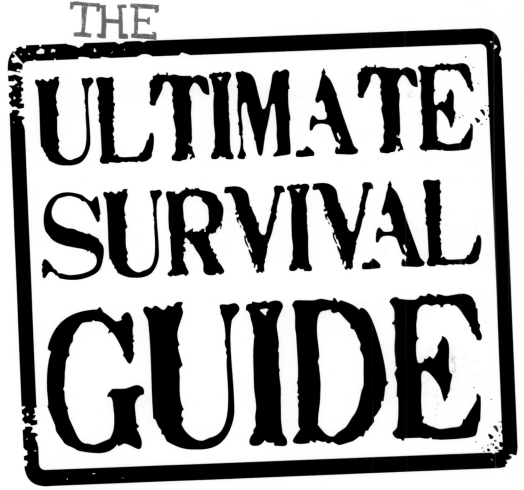

ULTIMATE SURVIVAL GUIDE

Mike Flynn

Illustrated by Mike Phillips
With an introduction by Ben Fogle

Macmillan Children's Books

First published 2008 by Macmillan Children's Books

This edition published 2010 by Macmillan Children's Books
a division of Macmillan Publishers Limited
20 New Wharf Road, London N1 9RR
Basingstoke and Oxford
Associated companies throughout the world
www.panmacmillan.com

ISBN 978-0-330-46725-4

1 3 5 7 9 8 6 4 2

A CIP catalogue record for this book is available from the British Library.

Typeset and designed by Matthew Kelly
Printed and bound in China

Picture credits:
C. SAPPA/De Agostini Picture Library/Getty Images Pages 57, 59, 65,
86 (top, middle and bottom), 89 (left and right), 111 (middle).
Science Photo Library Page 87 (top).

Contents

Introduction by Ben Fogle 2

Greetings, Survivor! 4

Chapter 1: What am I doing here? 8

Chapter 2: Be warm, stay cool (dude) 36

Chapter 3: Where can I find water? 60

Chapter 4: Food, glorious food 80

Chapter 5: Working together, staying in touch 106

Chapter 6: The Ultimate Survival Kit 122

Survival Quiz 132

Index 136

INTRODUCTION

by Ben Fogle

Imagine skiing for sixteen hours a day for weeks on end in temperatures of minus fifty degrees – so cold that all the hairs in your nose freeze and each breath turns to ice and then shatters.

How about sleeping in a thin hammock where your only protection from the tarantulas, snakes and jaguars that inhabit the jungle is a mosquito net that hangs between the dark, dank trees.

I love adventure and I've spent fifteen years exploring some of the most inhospitable places on earth.

I have trekked across the driest deserts, hacked across jungles and climbed some of the highest mountains in my quest to explore the world.

I have spent weeks paddling down anaconda and piranha infested rivers in South America in search of one of the highest waterfalls on the planet and gone in search of undiscovered tribes in Papua New Guinea.

I have trekked hundreds of miles across bogs and climbed icy mountain glaciers. I have been bitten by insects, spiders and ants and slept in countless hammocks and snow-holes all in pursuit of happiness and excitement.

I love sleeping under the trees, listing to the sound of nature all around and feeling close to the natural world and all its wonders.

I enjoy pushing physical and geographical boundaries and in doing so I have raced the notorious Marathon des Sables, a 150-mile foot race across the Sahara Desert, and I've spent

forty-nine days rowing 3000 miles across the Atlantic Ocean in a tiny twenty-foot long rowing boat. I've even spent a year living on a remote, windswept, uninhabited island with just a handful of people, like real-life Robinson Crusoes.

As a child I used to spend my summers in the Canadian wilderness. I'd build rafts, paddle canoes and make camps on the little islands that dotted the lakes. I'd catch fish in the clear waters and forage for berries in the forests.

I'd spend hours watching beavers and moose and loved being so close to nature. I always hoped that one day I might become an adventurer.

Most recently I skied 550 miles across Antarctica in a race to the South Pole. Pulling a sledge with all my food, tent and provisions I endured freezing temperatures, sleep deprivation and hunger in my quest to make it to the bottom of the world.

If you too love adventure and exploring, then why not begin with some wild camping – you can even use your garden. This book gives all budding adventurers plenty of handy hints and could help you become a real-life explorer.

GREETINGS, SURVIVOR!

Ever wondered what would happen if you were out on a day trip to a forest and got lost or separated from your friends or family? Or have you thought about how you might cope if you were in a plane crash and were the only survivor?

No one sets out to get lost or trapped in a dangerous place yet sometimes it happens. But while the world may seem like an awfully big and scary place it doesn't have to be so long as you've learned a few basic skills and developed some good, simple habits.

GET FIT

The first thing you can do to improve your chances of survival is the simplest but perhaps the most important. If you're not fit, then get fit. You don't have to go to the gym five times a week and you don't even have to play a team sport if that doesn't suit you. Just stay active. Do a few press-ups and sit-ups, kick a ball against a wall . . . anything so long as your heart rate is raised for at least half an hour a day, every day.

After all, you never know when you might need the strength this will bring you. If your school were to catch fire while you were in it, how long do you think you could hang from a top-floor window before someone could get a ladder to you and help you down? One minute? Two minutes? Ten minutes?

LEARN TO SWIM

If you can't swim, get someone to teach you; if you can swim, learn to do it better and for longer. Ask yourself, if you were on a ship that sank while far out at sea, how long could you tread water before help arrived? And if you were just a mile or so into your voyage, would you have the strength to swim back to the shore?

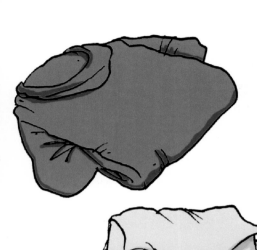

BE PREPARED

Carry enough clothing of the right sort for the climate you find yourself in. Yes, it's a pain to have to drag a coat around all day, but you'll be glad you did when darkness falls along with the temperature. And always try to wear solid, comfortable shoes or boots that you'd be able to walk – or run – a good few miles in.

Learn as much as you can about any new country you might be about to visit – and not just where the amusement parks and beaches are. Find out who you can call on in a crisis, where the rivers are and what kind of wildlife you can expect to encounter – especially the wildlife with big teeth or poisonous bites and stings.

The CIA has an amazing website (type 'CIA World Factbook' into a search engine) where you can discover much of the background information you'll ever need to know on just about every country in the world.

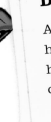

DID YOU KNOW?

About 70% of your total body heat can escape through your head, so always wear a hat on a cold day.

THE GOLDEN RULES OF SURVIVAL

In the rest of this book we'll look at the things you'll need to survive in all sorts of difficult and scary situations. But before we do here are a few golden rules that you should copy down and keep in your Ultimate Survival Kit (see Chapter 6).

1 If you are lost with a friend, stick together. You'll more than double your chances of survival. You can keep each other warm and tell the rudest jokes you know until someone comes and gets you.

2 Don't wander about. If you're completely lost in a forest, wandering around will reduce the chances of a rescue team finding you and increase your chances of having an accident. Your rescuers will search the forest a bit at a time so stay where you are and they will get to you eventually.

3 If it's cold, try to stay warm. Cover up as much as you can and make sure you wear a hat. If you haven't got a hat, try to make one – a plastic bag stuffed with dry leaves will do. If it's hot try to stay in the shade and keep any movement to a minimum.

4 Find or make a shelter. This should keep the weather out but you must remain visible enough for rescuers to be able to see you.

5 Build a signal fire or leave a sign – ideally visible from the air – for your rescuers to find. Remember: you're not hiding from the enemy, you're trying to contact a friend.

6 Don't eat anything you don't recognize. And even if you do recognize it only eat it if you are absolutely certain that it is safe to do so. Although you'll end up feeling very hungry, you should be able to survive without food for a surprisingly long time.

7 Drink water – this is vital. See Chapter 3 for more information on this.

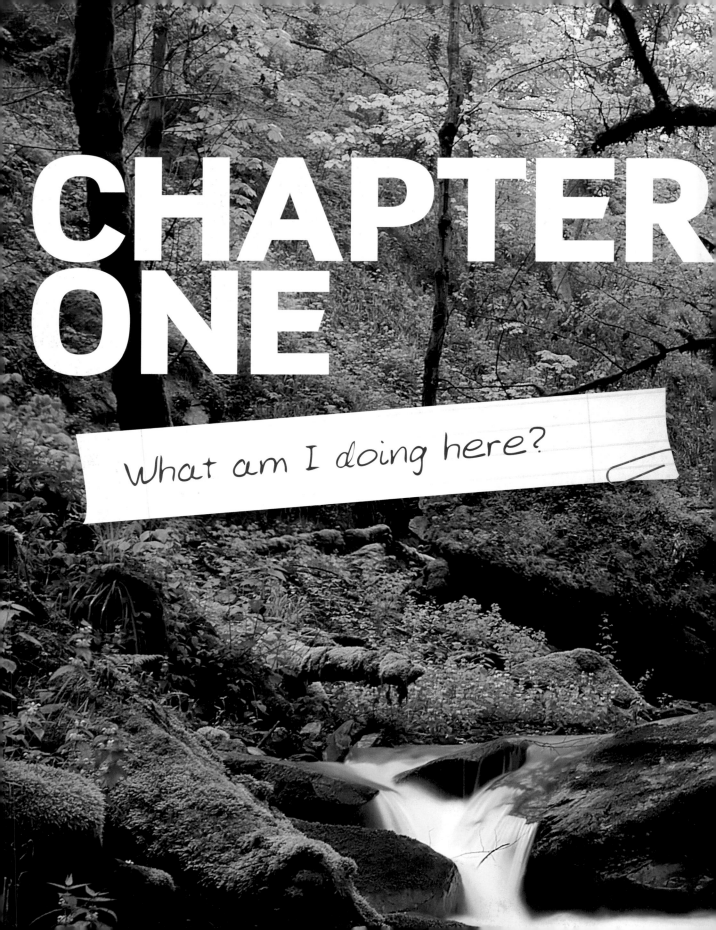

CHAPTER ONE

What am I doing here?

WHAT AM I DOING HERE?

OK. You're lost. Your stomach is turning over, your mind is racing, your palms begin to sweat, everything suddenly looks a bit spooky and scary and you wish, you really wish, you'd stayed at home and done nothing more adventurous than kill aliens, crash cars and conquer strange new worlds on your oh-so-safe games console. What should you do?

Well, first of all do nothing. Not a thing. Then take a deep breath. And another one. Now calm down and try to relax.

Look, it's not that bad. You got to where you are without meeting anything big and nasty. It wasn't scary on the way in — otherwise you probably wouldn't have walked in without paying attention — and, anyway, trolls, ogres and witches are mostly vegetarian these days, so you'll have little to fear from them.

TOP TIP

Always let someone know where you are going and how long you expect to be out for. That way, you'll always have backup if something goes wrong. After all, you might be a highly skilled outdoorsman but that's going to be of no use when you trip over a tree root and knock yourself unconscious.

WHERE AM I?

You mean you don't remember? Shame on you! Whenever you head into the unknown you must make a point of keeping your eyes open. This might seem like an obvious thing to say, but it's surprising just how many people come unstuck simply because they haven't bothered to make a note of the landscape they've been passing through.

As you walk along, make a mental checklist of any interesting features you see. How many trees did you spy in the middle of that small clearing? What was the ground doing: was it smooth and flat, rising or falling, muddy or firm? Are there any man-made features, such as an abandoned farm building, perhaps, or an old bit of fence?

Listen out for clues as well. Perhaps you heard a car driving along a nearby road. Did you hear any trains? Can you hear a waterfall?

Making a note of things like these can save your life.

TOP TIP

Landscapes often look different when seen from another angle. Every now and then, stop and look behind you so you'll have a better chance of recognizing where you've been when you return.

11

SHOULD I STAY OR SHOULD I GO?

Sometimes the best thing you can do is stay pretty much exactly where you are. Chances are that if someone knows roughly where to find you they will eventually form a search party and come looking for you. (You did tell someone you were planning on going out alone, didn't you?)

How well do you know the area? If you know you're in a small forest surrounded by farmland, then you could probably walk in almost any direction and eventually find a farmhouse, a road and perhaps even a bus home.

But be careful. Even in densely populated countries you might find yourself walking twenty miles or so before accidentally stumbling across civilization.

If, however, you are on the edge of a true wilderness, such as the Rocky Mountains, the Sahara Desert, or the edge of the Amazon Jungle, you could walk for hundreds of miles and never see another human being. Ever again.

So, as they say in the north of England, 'If in doubt, do nowt.'

WHAT NOW?

It's at times like this that a compass can come in very handy. A normal compass is really just a magnetized needle that always points north. The needle is balanced on a fine point called a pivot, which allows it to turn in any direction.

This means that finding your way north should be a doddle – just follow the arrow. Want to go south? Walk the opposite way. East? Simply keep the arrow pointing to your left. West? Make sure the arrow is pointing to your right.

Dead simple, really.

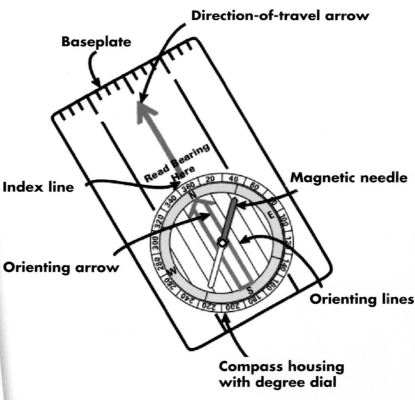

Direction-of-travel arrow

Baseplate

Read Bearing Here

Index line

Magnetic needle

Orienting arrow

Orienting lines

Compass housing with degree dial

Activity

MAKE A SIMPLE COMPASS

You can make a simple compass at home using a sewing needle, a piece of a drinking straw a tiny bit shorter than the needle, a piece of silk or a magnet, and a bowl of water.

A SEWING NEEDLE **STRAW** **PIECE OF SILK** **BOWL OF WATER**

1 Carefully rub the needle in one direction only with the piece of silk or magnet – this makes the needle magnetic.

2 Put the needle inside the straw, so that it will float.

DID YOU KNOW?

There is some evidence that the Chinese were using a compass-like instrument around 2,000 years ago.

3 Gently put the straw on the surface of the water and then watch in amazement as the needle lines up with the Earth's magnetic field.

THE EARTH'S MAGNETIC FIELD

Metallic elements near the Earth's core, combined with the Earth's rotation, generate a truly huge magnetic field which stretches thousands of miles out into space. Not only does this protect us from the worst effects of the sun's radiation – without the magnetic field there'd be no life on Earth – it also means that we have a reliable way of finding our way around.

As we know from our compasses, any magnetic metal will, when left to turn freely, position itself along a north-to-south line in keeping with its position in the magnetic field.

DID YOU KNOW?

The magnetic north and south poles are not in quite the same places as the actual North and South Poles. This is because the magnetic poles move around a little from time to time, probably because of changes at the Earth's core.

DESERT NAVIGATION

These days you're as likely to see the Bedouin (nomadic Arabs) riding in a 4x4 as you are to see them on a camel. But they retain their old skills and can still, if called upon, find their way around without the aid of satellite navigation systems, which is just as well, as the shifting sands of the desert present all kinds of difficult navigational problems.

Eventually the clear skies of the day will give way to the wondrous spectacle of the night sky over the desert. It is surely no wonder that the Arab world gave us so many of the early astronomers. They had an almost unparalleled view of the heavens, which they were among the first to chart, and they very quickly learned to navigate by using the North Star. This is why, unless you have a compass, you should always travel in the desert at night.

HOW TO FIND THE NORTH STAR

From our position here on Earth, the stars in the night sky seem to move over the course of several hours. In reality, it takes around a quarter of a billion years for the Milky Way Galaxy, home of all the stars you can see in the night sky, to rotate. The illusion of movement is caused by the fact that the

Earth rotates once every twenty-four hours on its year-long journey around the sun.

However, there is one star, directly over the North Pole, which appears to remain rooted to the spot. Once you've identified this star, known as the North Star or Pole Star, you can then be sure which way north lies and, with a little thought, figure out where to find south, east and west and all points in between.

To find the North Star look out for the Big Dipper (which is also known as the Plough, because of its plough-like shape). Join up the stars in your imagination to make a plough shape (there are no lines drawn in the real night sky), then continue in a straight line until you hit the tip of what is known as the Little Dipper, which looks a little like a scoop. This star is the North Star and directly below it lies the North Pole.

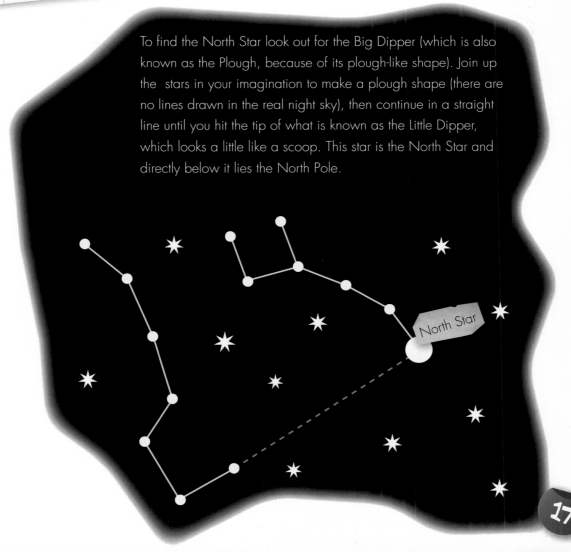

North Star

17

HOW TO FIND SOUTH USING THE STARS

Wouldn't it be handy if there was a 'South Star' to match the North Star? Alas, we've no such luck. There is a very faint star in roughly that position, but on a clear dark night it would be far too easy to pick out the wrong one from among all of the other, far brighter stars in that part of the sky. So instead we have to rely on two other groups of stars and three hands.

In the southern hemisphere, look out for two very bright stars, which are known to explorers as the Pointers. Draw a line up through them in your imagination and continue until you reach the famous Southern Cross – so called because it's in the southern sky and it's shaped like a cross.

Follow the longest part of the cross down with your eyes and, holding your hands up at arm's length, measure out three hand-spans to the right across the sky. Now look vertically down from about the base of your little finger. The point where your eye meets the horizon will be due south.

Be warned, however, that this is only a very rough way of figuring out due south. If at all possible try to confirm your position by other means, such as a compass, or you may end up getting horribly lost.

SOUTHERN CROSS

POINTERS

CANOPUS

SOUTH CELESTIAL POLE

ACHEMAR

SOUTH

HORIZON

HOW TO READ A MAP

Funnily enough, it's very easy to get lost when reading a map. But a map is really just a set of directions to pretty much anywhere you'd like to go with the added bonus of extra information about the kind of land you'll be crossing and some interesting features you might encounter along the way.

Aside from rivers and lakes, which are indicated in blue, the most important feature for you to look out for on a map is the contour lines. These are the wobbly lines that cover most maps and are used to give some idea of the shape of the land. Where the lines are far apart the land will be relatively flat, but when they are drawn very close together you can be sure that you'll have to cross a steep landscape.

Normal people avoid these bits, but climbers, fell runners and other adventurers tend to go looking for them.

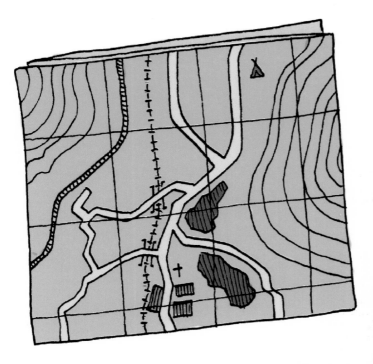

ROAD
RIVER
RAILWAY LINE
RAILWAY TUNNEL
PLACE OF WORSHIP
CAMPSITE
WOODLAND
BUILT-UP AREA
HIGHER GROUND

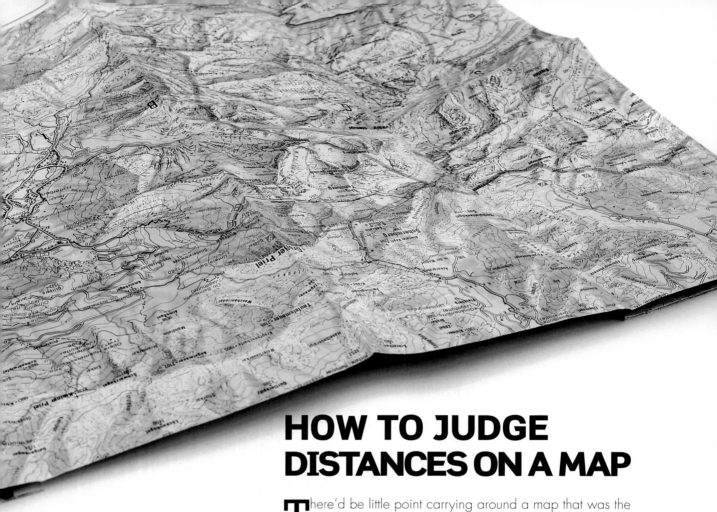

HOW TO JUDGE DISTANCES ON A MAP

There'd be little point carrying around a map that was the same size as the actual area you wanted to navigate around. Because of this, most maps are drawn to scale. For example, a scale of 1:22,000 indicates that 4.55 cm on the map is equal to 1 km.

Not very clear, though, is it?

So here's a really cool trick. Instead of doing lots of calculations, place your thumb over a recognizable feature on the map, such as the stretch of river bank from which you might be starting your great big adventure, and then pace out the distance covered by your thumb.

Starting with the right foot, walk the distance covered by your thumb on the map while counting out the number of times your left foot hits the ground — each time your left foot hits the ground you will have covered a full pace.

When you reach the end of the distance covered by your thumb – perhaps 100 paces – you'll have a much better sense of the distances indicated on your map. How far away is that hill? Oooh, about ten thumbs' worth – a thousand paces.

This can make life much easier and also give you a sense of where things really are in relation to your position.

FOLLOWING A HEADING

You may have heard expressions like 'heading in the right direction' or 'heading for trouble'. Both of these expressions have their origins in the art of navigation. To take a heading, i.e. decide on the direction you would like to follow, first hold your compass level so that the needle can move freely.

Once you've figured out which way north lies, decide which direction you would like to go. Now try to spot a landmark that lies in that direction, some distance away and yet easy to spot. This might be a distinctive peak or perhaps a very large tree sitting near the top of a hill.

Finished? Well done, you've just taken a heading. Now, put your compass safely away and make your way towards the feature that you picked out.

Once you get there, repeat the two steps outlined above, i.e. check your compass, pick a landmark along the heading you wish to travel and make your way towards it. Keep repeating these two steps until you get to where you want to go.

The beauty of this approach is that it saves you the bother of having to keep referring back to your compass and it allows you to take in far more of your surroundings. This means that you can find your way back easily, avoid stepping off cliffs and keep an eye out for wolves, tigers or groups of elderly tourists in bright red anoraks who can't find their way back to their coach – but are often a surprisingly generous source of sweeties.

LATITUDE, LONGITUDE AND ATTITUDE

If you look closely at a map of the world you'll notice that it's criss-crossed with horizontal and vertical lines. The horizontal lines are called lines of latitude. They measure off the distance from the equator, an imaginary line that runs like a very long belt around the middle of the Earth.

The vertical lines radiate out from the North to the South Pole and are called lines of longitude. They give a measure, in

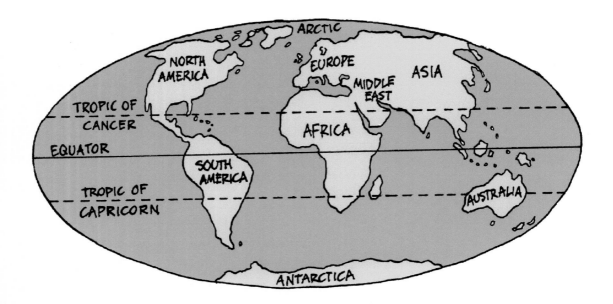

degrees, of the distance from an imaginary line called the prime meridian. This is also called zero longitude and runs through a delightful village in London called Greenwich, home of the *Cutty Sark* and any number of cosy if rather crowded pubs and cafes.

Why Greenwich? WHY NOT! (That was the attitude bit.)

DEGREES OF SEPARATION

Latitude and longitude are both measured in degrees, which have their very own symbol. It looks like this: ° (OK not too impressive but we're stuck with it). The map of the world is divided up into degrees of latitude and degrees of longitude.

Each individual degree is then further divided up into sixty minutes, which have a far from impressive symbol that looks like this: '. And as if that wasn't enough, each individual minute is then further divided up into sixty seconds, which are indicated with a symbol that looks like this: ". (You there, at the back, are you keeping up?)

All of this allows us to give a pinpoint accurate description of where we are on the surface of the Earth just by stating our latitude and longitude. For example, I am writing this at latitude 51° 29' 53" North 0° 10' 27" West. If you know where you are to within a single second you'll make life a lot simpler for anyone trying to rescue you – the last thing a mountain rescue team wants to hear when they ask where you are is 'On a mountain'.

GPS

GPS stands for Global Positioning System. A GPS unit is just about the best thing ever invented in the history of navigation. It's really a very clever form of radio which calls up a spider's web of satellites placed in orbit above the Earth and uses information provided by four or five of them to figure out precisely where you are. This information is then displayed as a set of coordinates - your latitude and longitude - on the GPS unit's screen. All you have to do is look these up on your map and you'll know exactly where you are.

But what happens when the batteries run out, or you drop and break the unit, or – how embarrassing – you realize you let it fall out of your pocket when you were tying up your boots a couple of miles back?

This is when basic skills with a map and compass can come in very handy. A GPS unit is a wonderful thing, but if you're going to carry one make sure that you always, ALWAYS have a compass with you as well.

WHAT IS GPS?

There are twenty-four satellites making up the worldwide radio-navigation global positioning system. They orbit the earth every twelve hours in a formation that ensures that every point on earth will be able to make radio contact with at least four satellites. The satellites transmit radio signals. These are picked up and interpreted by a receiver, which calculates co-ordinates accurate to within 1cm.

THE BEAUFORT SCALE

How windy is windy? Recognizing that one man's gust is another man's gale, British Admiral Sir Francis Beaufort drew up a table of wind speeds in 1805. This divided up a broad spectrum of wind conditions – from 'barely a flicker' to 'drop the sails and start to pray' – laid out on a scale from zero to Force 12.

Forces 13 to 17 were added later to take into account typhoons in the South China Seas, but these remain in use only in that part of the world.

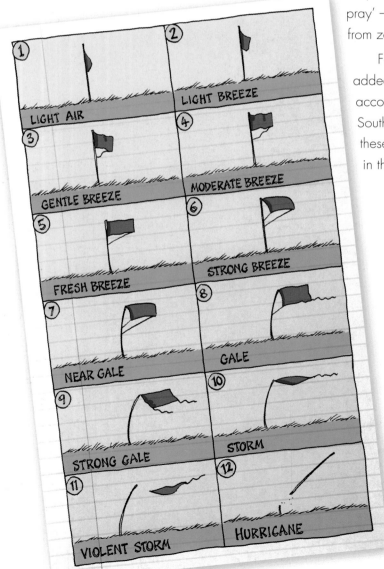

1 LIGHT AIR
2 LIGHT BREEZE
3 GENTLE BREEZE
4 MODERATE BREEZE
5 FRESH BREEZE
6 STRONG BREEZE
7 NEAR GALE
8 GALE
9 STRONG GALE
10 STORM
11 VIOLENT STORM
12 HURRICANE

READING THE WEATHER

Despite what the weather forecasters might like you to think, predicting the weather is not an exact science – although it is a surprisingly expensive one. In truth, it's closer to alchemy or astrology than to real science, but it's still possible to make a few general predictions based on your own observations.

The most famous saying about the weather is 'Red sky at night, shepherds' delight; red sky at morning, shepherds take warning', which still stands as a reasonable guide to the coming weather.

The sky appears red because of the effects of sunlight passing through clouds at a shallow angle, caused by the sun dropping below the horizon either as it goes down at night (in the west) or rises in the morning (in the east). This means that a red sky at night indicates that rain clouds are moving away from you (in the direction of the setting sun). When red skies appear in the morning this means that rain is on its way towards you and you should find some shelter or prepare to get wet.

If you want to know what the weather is likely to be doing tomorrow, or the day after, you can check on the TV, in a newspaper or on a website. The weather for the coming days is usually presented with symbols (called icons) showing what kind of conditions you can expect. There are often numbers given for the highest, lowest and average expected temperatures, plus a shining sun if it's going to be sunny, rain clouds and rain if it's going to be rainy, and so on.

MON	TUE	WED	THUR	FRI
PARTLY CLOUDY	MOSTLY CLOUDY	RAIN	RAIN	SUNNY
74°	73°	71°	71°	75°
56°	57°	55°	56°	57°

VIKING NAVIGATION

Back in the days when men had really tough names like Bloodaxe, Hardrada, Forkbeard and Jeremy, the Vikings were using a simple sun compass to navigate across vast stretches of the world. There are records of them visiting places as far south as Africa, as far east as Russia and Turkey and as far west as parts of America. They would have gone north as well, but they lived there already. That's how they got the name Norsemen, which literally means 'men from the north'.

DID YOU KNOW?

Although they would if they could, polar bears don't eat penguins. This is because polar bears live around the Arctic (north) and penguins live around the Antarctic (south). They're literally a world apart!

How to make a sun compass

To make this simple compass all you will need is a long stick, four large flat stones, a marker pen and a watch.

1 First of all, fix the stick in the ground so that it points straight up. At exactly midday the sun will be shining on you from the south (in the northern hemisphere) This means that any shadow the stick casts will be pointing north. Follow the shadow and place the first of your four large stones along this line, having first written a great big N (for 'north') on it.

2 Now place another stone on the exact opposite side of the stick from the 'N' stone and write a great big S (for 'south') on it. While facing north, you should then place the two remaining stones, marked W for 'west' and E for 'east' on the left and right of the stick, at the same distance from the centre as the other two stones.

3 You should now have a fairly accurate sun compass, which indicates the four main points for navigation.

How to use your wristwatch as a compass

So long as it is showing the correct time, you can use your wristwatch as a compass. This is no substitute for a real compass but will give you a good idea of where to find south and from there all the other points on the compass.

You will need:

- A traditional dial-faced wristwatch that shows the correct time
- The sun
- A matchstick or straight blade of grass

Step by step

1. Hold your watch out flat, face up, in front of you.

2. Position the watch so that the hour hand points at the sun.

3. Place the matchstick or straight blade of grass across the watch so that it passes exactly through the middle of the watch face.

4. Keeping the hour hand lined up with the sun, move the match so that the end with the tip lies halfway between the hour hand and the number 12. The match will now be pointing directly south.

Why it works

The Earth rotates once every twenty-four hours, giving the impression that the sun rises in the east and sets in the west. The sun also, when seen from the northern hemisphere, appears to move across the southern sky. By taking into account the amount of time it has been travelling across the sky (which is why you need a wristwatch), you can figure out which way due south lies.

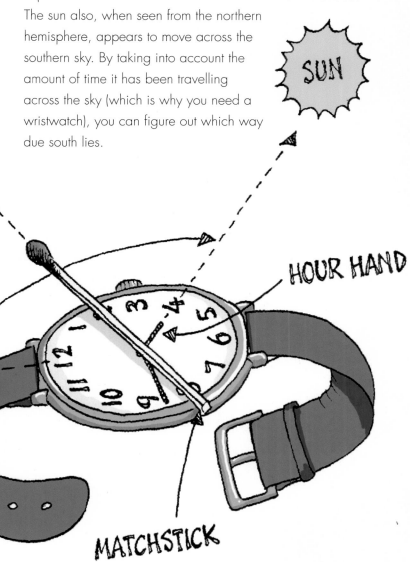

SUN

SOUTH

HOUR HAND

MATCHSTICK

Activity

How to make a treasure map

One of the best ways to learn how to use a map is to make one yourself. You'll soon discover what you should be looking for in a map and quickly figure out what is, and isn't, of importance.

Here is an example of a simple treasure map. Why not make one of your own and see if your friends can follow it to the treasure (which needn't be made up of gold and jewels)?

Survival Story

If only he'd let someone know where he was going . . .

Dr Ellis Webster goes on a fishing trip he'll never forget.

October 6, 1993, will stay in Dr Ellis Webster's memory for the rest of his life. For this was the day that his world changed forever as a result of the most basic survival error - he didn't bother to tell anyone where he was going.

Dr Webster, an American surgeon, decided to get away from it all for a few hours by going fishing down at a small lake near St Mary's Glacier, just a few miles outside the large American city of Denver. He'd very sensibly checked the weather and knew that a severe snow-storm was predicted for that evening. Naturally he wasn't planning on staying out very long.

For this reason, he hadn't bothered to bring any extra clothing, food or even the means to make a fire. Why would he? He wasn't going to need them as he planned to be home before dark.

But fate had other plans for Dr Webster, plans that would require some of his surgical skills and all of his extraordinary courage. Before the day was over, the good doctor was going to have to make one of the toughest choices that any of us may ever have to face.

For here was an intelligent man who had done a very stupid thing, and while he may well have got away with it ninety-nine times out of a hundred, today would be the one day he would be held to account for his actions in the cruellest possible way. And it all began with a minor accident.

As the doctor was making his way down to the lake, he slipped a little before tripping and falling over. No big deal, except that as he fell he pushed against a large boulder. While he was still lying on the ground the boulder moved, landing on his left leg, crushing it beyond use and trapping him where he lay.

Slowly, cold terror settled upon the doctor. He knew he was trapped. He realized that no one knew where to find him and he felt, with absolute certainty, that unless by some freak chance rescue were to arrive before nightfall he was going to freeze to death trapped under the boulder and the rapidly falling snow.

What follows is not for the faint-hearted. If you're at all squeamish don't read any further: you have been warned!

The one chance Dr Webster had of survival lay in his fishing tackle box, which he could just reach from where he lay. Removing the pocket knife he kept in the box, Dr Webster put his considerable surgical skills to work . . . on himself.

First he tied a length of fishing line very tightly around his thigh - in order to reduce the bleeding that would soon follow. Then, and without the aid of any sort of painkiller, he began to saw through his own leg. After first slicing away at the skin, he cut the tendons, nerves and ligaments above the knee. Once he had cut through all of the parts holding his leg on he finally began pulling and sliding his femur (thigh bone) out from his knee joint.

34

It's impossible to imagine the kind of pain he must have been in at this point. Any experienced hunter who has set a snare for a rabbit will tell you that these poor creatures will sometimes bite their own leg off in order to escape from a trap. But how often are humans called upon to make this horrifying sacrifice?

Yet Dr Webster found the courage to do what needed to be done. Faced with the possibility of bleeding to death, or the absolute certainty of freezing to death, he took the 'best' option he had and chose to live.

Amazingly, once free, he had to drag himself just half a mile to find help, and an air ambulance was called to take him to the University of Colorado Hospital in Denver. His leg was later recovered by the rescue team, but was so badly damaged after being amputated by a fishing tackle knife that his surgical colleagues were unable to reattach it.

To this day Dr Ellis Webster continues to walk about, but on an artificial leg. He has recovered well from his horrific ordeal but no longer wants to talk about it. Of course, if he had bothered to tell someone where he was going in the first place, then none of this would have happened. Eventually, someone would have noticed that he was missing and would have raised the alarm.

Don't end up like Dr Webster. Always let someone know where you are going.

CHAPTER TWO

Be warm, stay cool (dude)

BE WARM, STAY COOL (DUDE)

You might be brave, but you – and all the rest of us – are really rather delicate. We can cope with a certain amount of heat and a small amount of cold, but the moment the thermometer shifts too far either way we very quickly find ourselves in trouble.

WE MAKE THE WORLD FIT US

Fortunately, because we are by far the cleverest monkeys on the planet we have learned to adapt our surroundings to suit ourselves. This makes us unlike every other animal on Earth, which must evolve to fit its surroundings.

This is why we have a duty to protect all of these other creatures. They can't turn the central heating on when things get a bit chilly, or build a boat and row to safety when a flood comes. Instead, many of them get cold and die, or get wet and drown.

But we were born lucky. In cold places we can wear thick woolly jumpers and big warm coats and boots and drink hot chocolate by the fire that we made in the shelter that we built. In hot places we can put on sun hats and sunscreen and sit in deckchairs in the shade, drinking tall cool drinks with lots of ice.

In fact, we've come so far in the last 30,000 years or so that, with the help of sealed buildings and air conditioning, we can build cities in deserts. We even have the technology to live on the Moon or planet Mars – though it's unlikely that you'll be able to go out and play in the park when you get there.

WHAT IS A SAFE TEMPERATURE FOR ME?

The temperature at which your body works best, and at which you'll feel most comfortable, is 37 °C. Under normal circumstances your body will very cleverly do all it can to keep you at this temperature no matter how hot or how cold your surroundings might be.

Getting a little warm? You'll soon find yourself sweating. Feeling a little chilly? Here come the goosebumps and shivers. In fact, your breathing patterns, sweating, blood circulation and even the speed at which you move will be controlled by your brain in an attempt to maintain this ideal temperature.

But sometimes your body's systems become overworked. Heat from the sun, or perhaps the heat you generate by doing too much exercise, can cause your body to reach a point where your natural systems can't cope. Sometimes the effects can be quite mild – you might get a sweaty rash – but other times they can be life-threatening.

WHAT HAPPENS IF I GET TOO HOT?

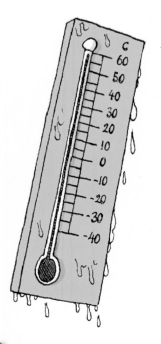

As you get warmer your skin will start to sweat. It will carry on doing this for as long as you have enough fluids in your body. When these start to run out you will soon be heading for trouble, or hyperthermia as doctors like to call it. (Hyperthermia, meaning over-heated, is the opposite of hypothermia, which is the name doctors give to the problem of getting too cold.)

You'll be OK with a rise in temperature of a couple of degrees but when your body's core temperature rises above 40 °C you will be in serious trouble.

Just a couple of degrees above this temperature and your brain will very slowly start to die. Another few degrees and you will almost certainly be dead from heatstroke. Not a good day.

HOW WILL I KNOW WHEN I'M IN TROUBLE?

Don't worry. Heatstroke hardly ever happens without some kind of warning. To start with you'll get really hot and confused and may even throw up. You'll probably notice at least one of these symptoms. At this point you should really take the hint and very quickly find a way of cooling down.

There's more information on the early warning signs of dehydration which often accompanies heatstroke, in Chapter 3.

Hat

Loose-fitting shirt

Loose-fitting shorts

Boots

HOW CAN I AVOID HEATSTROKE?

One of the best ways to avoid heatstroke is to hang loose and stay cool, dude. Wear lightweight, loose-fitting clothing that will allow air to circulate around your body and let your sweat evaporate – sweating is your body's really clever way of keeping you cool but it won't work unless you let air flow over your skin.

You could be really cool and get yourself a hat. Why not get a stetson? People will think you're a cowboy and it will keep your head cool, plus the wide brim will keep the sun off your face. Failing that, just about any light-coloured, lightweight broad-brimmed hat will do.

Obviously, it's a good idea to avoid doing any kind of hard physical work during the hottest part of the day (between about midday and 4 p.m.). And it goes without saying that you should also drink lots of water, even if you don't feel especially thirsty.

HOW CAN I TREAT HEATSTROKE IF MY FRIEND GOES DOWN WITH IT?

If your friend collapses from heat-stroke the very first thing you should do is call out the emergency services if you can do so quickly and easily. Either way you should immediately get to work on reducing your friend's temperature.

If you're out in the sun, move immediately into the shade. Remove any excess clothing and fan the body to promote cooling. Place cool, wet towels (or T-shirts) around the head, neck and torso but don't try to cool your friend down too quickly. (So, no ice packs just yet.) If you're near water, such as the sea or a cool river, place your friend in it, but only if they have not passed out.

Try to get as much fluid into your friend as possible, but keep an eye on their condition while doing this. (Some people feel that fluids should only be given by emergency personnel under these circumstances, but if there aren't any handy you will have no choice but to do it yourself.)

If your friend is unconscious, do all you can to make sure that their airways are kept clear.

STAYING COOL IN THE DESERT

The Bedouin used to travel everywhere either on foot or on camels, trailing goats and sheep behind them. Naturally, they would use wool made from the hair of these animals to make some of their clothing as well as their blankets and even their tents. Some of these items could be traded to buy cotton.

Bedouin men traditionally stay cool by wearing a long, loose-fitting white tunic made of cotton. On their heads they wear a distinctive head cloth called a 'kufiyya'. This is held on by a kind of headband called an 'agal'. The kufiyya can be wrapped around the face and neck to shield the wearer from the sun. It also helps to keep out sand, which can be a real problem when the desert winds start to blow.

The women wear a long black tunic called a 'bourque', which covers the head, face and body. This protects the wearer from the strong rays of the sun and does an excellent job of keeping out the sand.

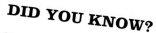

STAYING COOL
IN THE JUNGLE

You can't stay cool in the jungle, fool. Get used to it. Wear lightweight, breathable fabrics, strong boots with high sides – so the snakes will have something to chew on that isn't you – and a good hat. The canopy formed by the trees and other plants will probably protect your head from the sun, but it's always a good idea to carry a hat. It won't actually make you any cooler but it might just make you look cool.

And now we go from one extreme to another . . .

I'M FREEZING TO DEATH! WHAT'S GOING ON?

When your core body temperature drops a couple of degrees below 37 °C you will get goosebumps and start to shiver. This isn't usually a big problem as you can often simply jump up and down a bit or do a few press-ups to raise your temperature back to a safe level.

But as you get colder you'll find that the shivering gets more and more violent. Your body's extremities will start to turn blue as your brain diverts blood away from these bits to the vital organs in your torso – your heart, lungs, etc.

Another few degrees colder and you will be in very serious trouble. Even though you don't feel any warmer, you'll stop shivering. This is the first sign that something is horribly wrong. You'll become confused and you won't be able to operate a phone or fasten a button or zip.

As your heart gets colder it will start to beat more and more slowly, which means that your brain and other organs simply won't be getting enough oxygen. Before you know it, most of your internal organs will fail and you'll be clinically dead.

45

FROSTBITE

Jack Frost may nip at your toes but frostbite will chew them off and spit them out. Once the outside temperature drops below freezing, the tiny blood vessels close to the surface of your skin will start to narrow. This is your brain's way of keeping your heart warm and in the short term it will do you no harm. However, in those parts of your body that are furthest from your heart – such as your nose, fingers and toes – too much cold, combined with the reduced blood flow, can cause the skin and muscles to become damaged.

Eventually, the skin in these exposed bits will turn black, which is a sure sign that the nerves and blood vessels below the skin are severely damaged. Soon a condition called gangrene will follow, which will mean that these bits will have to be cut off.

At this point you'll probably wish you'd worn your gloves when you set off on your adventure.

MY FRIEND IS FREEZING TO DEATH. WHAT CAN I DO?

Long before either of you gets this cold, you should have attempted to call out the emergency services. Assuming you have, the very next thing you should do is find some form of temporary shelter and then get to work on increasing your friend's temperature.

If you have the means to build and start a fire, do so straight away and, if possible, make them (and yourself) a hot drink. Also make sure they are not lying on anything really cold, such as the ground. Then put any spare clothing you have on your friend, but keep on any clothing that is keeping you warm – there's no point in both of you dying.

Remember that it's very important to keep the body's core temperature as close to normal as possible, even if this means sacrificing a finger or three. That said, try to keep your friend's hands, feet, face and, most importantly, head warm. If you have a rucksack or something similar, empty it out and put their feet in it. It will trap a little more heat than shoes or boots alone. It's also vitally important to keep your friend awake at all times – most people who freeze to death do so after they lose consciousness. Then get up close and personal. (This is no time to be shy!) Cosying up together will allow you to share any spare body heat you have with your friend. Even the super-tough SAS do this, and it might just keep the pair of you alive until help arrives.

STAYING WARM
IN THE ARCTIC

The Inuit (native people of the Artic region) used to keep themselves warm with a combination of animal skins, furs and very, very fatty food. But in recent years there have been amazing improvements in the quality of man-made fabrics, which are now much better at keeping us warm and dry than just about any combination of fur and fat.

Most Arctic clothing is made from a mixture of water-resistant and water-transferring (also called high-wicking) fibres. The underwear layer closest to the skin is a pair of long johns (ask your grandad) made of a high-wicking fabric that draws sweat away from the body. This is topped by a lightweight fleece top and trousers. This does the same job, only more so.

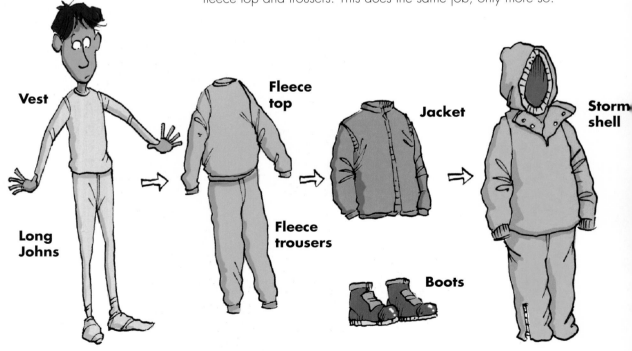

Vest

Long Johns

Fleece top

Fleece trousers

Jacket

Boots

Storm shell

Next a jacket is added. This will have zips around the armpits which can be opened for extra ventilation, weather permitting. A layer made of very fine tightly woven fabric is designed to slow down the rate at which your body loses moisture. Finally, the whole outfit is covered in a storm shell. This is made of a very hardwearing fabric which lets sweat out but stops any kind of moisture coming in. The feet are protected by flexible boots constructed from man-made materials but more often than not lined with animal fur.

DID YOU KNOW?

A sled pulled by a team of dogs is still one of the best ways of getting around the Arctic. But these days even the dogs wear little fur-lined booties to stop their feet getting cold!

FIRE IS OUR FRIEND

In most survival situations a fire is pretty much essential if you plan on staying alive. It can keep you warm, let you boil water, cook your food and scare off beasties (it's only pet dogs that like to be in front of a fire).

A fire needs three things: fuel, flames and oxygen. The fuel is provided by wood, twigs, leaves and whatever else you can find that will burn. The flames can be started by setting light to tinder. This is generally light dry pieces of wood and leaves that you can find on the ground, or specially prepared firelighters. Finally, the oxygen is supplied by the air around us (twenty-one per cent of which is made up of oxygen).

TOP TIP

If you don't have any firelighters but are near a pine tree you can gather the resin which drips out from the bark of the tree on a handful of twigs and use these instead. Pine resin is very, very flammable, which is why you should be especially careful about putting out any fires that you light in a forest.

How to make a tepee fire

With very little effort you can make a simple tepee fire which will keep you warm and scare off our fanged friends.

Take six logs and arrange them in the shape of a Native American tepee (a sort of cone-shaped tent), placing them so that they meet at the top and stand firmly together. Now fill the space underneath them with lots of tinder and kindling (kindling is like tinder only bigger).

Light the tinder and blow gently in the glowing embers until you see flames. Replace the logs as and when they burn down.

TEPEE

How to make an A-frame fire

Another simple fire design is the A-frame. Arrange your logs in the shape of a triangle. Build up a couple of layers following this pattern and pile up tinder and kindling in the centre. When ready, light the tinder and prepare to get warm.

The gaps you create between the logs will allow oxygen to rush through the fire, feeding the flames.

A-FRAME

PUTTING OUT YOUR FIRE

Never, ever leave a fire burning, even if it is only smouldering a little. To be absolutely certain that you've put out your fire follow these simple steps:

1. Kick over any remaining logs and spread them out.

2. Pour a bucket (or similar amount) of water over the remains of your fire.

3. If you are certain that the fire has gone out, touch the remaining logs and see if they still feel hot. If you feel any heat, pour more water over the logs.

4. Cover the remains of your fire in soil before adding more water. Your fire should now be well and truly out.

TYPES OF SHELTER

There are many different types of shelter, some of which occur naturally and others which can be bought, e.g. a tent, or built from things you might find lying around.

CAVE

SLIT TRENCH

GRASS BLANKET

Natural shelter

Caves, overhanging rock faces, hollow trees and wadis (dried-up riverbeds) can all be adapted to provide shelter from the elements. The simplest way of securing a cave, for example, is to build your fire at the entrance. This will keep most of the smoke out of the cave and deter any hungry animals from trying to get in.

LEAF AND BRANCH SHELTER

Adapted shelter

A slit trench, a leaf and branch shelter, a grass blanket and even a huge pile of horse manure are all examples of shelters that can be built by adapting the things around us. A slit trench, which is a bit like an open shallow grave, can be dug quite simply and then covered over with a sheet of plastic to make a basic shelter. A leaf and branch shelter, which is made by weaving and tying branches together in a criss-cross pattern, can also be used to cover the slit trench.

A grass blanket works well on dry nights. Cut the turf along one side and then extend the cut underneath the topsoil before hollowing it out to provide a natural sleeping bag – think pitta bread.

Horse manure, when left piled up, releases heat as it decomposes. This process can keep you warm all night . . . but only if you are prepared to bury yourself in the pile.

HUGE PILE OF MANURE

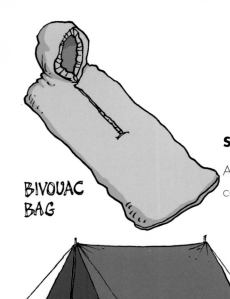

BIVOUAC
BAG

Shop-bought shelter

As well as tents, which are available in just about any combination of shape, size and colour you can imagine, one can also buy bivouac bags. These are a bit like a cross between an anorak and a sleeping bag. They provide cover for most of the body, leaving a small gap for breathing, and as long as you can find some sort of natural shelter from the wind and rain, such as a cave or an overhanging rock, they will keep you warm all night.

Desert shelter

Apart from wadis there is very little shelter to be found in the desert. Because of this the Bedouin carry their shelter with them in the form of large, heavy-duty tents made from densely-woven camel hair and vegetable fibres. On the very rare occasions when it rains in the desert, the fibres expand and stop any rain from getting through. The tents are held up with flexible poles and held down with strong guy ropes.

Traditionally, it is the women who put up the tents, which are divided into two 'rooms'. One room is called the *mag'ad*, which means 'sitting room'. This is reserved for the men and their guests. The other room is called the *ma'hamara*, and is reserved for the women and for cooking.

Survival Story: Stranded on the ice

This story is one of courage, bravery and, as is so often the case in the run-up to survival situations, stupidity.

On 12 May 1926, the airship *Norge* (meaning 'Norway') flew over the North Pole, the first time anyone had succeeded in making this journey in a lighter-than-air craft. The mission was led by Roald Amundsen, who in 1911 had beaten the tragic Captain Scott in the race to the South Pole. Now he could add this further triumph to his list of achievements, claiming the air record for the trip to the North Pole on behalf of his native Norway.

So far so good, except that the pilot of the airship, an Italian aviator by the name of Umberto Nobile, felt that the record should go to Italy, not least because he had provided the skill needed to fly the ship to its destination. When he didn't get his way, he decided to stage a second mission, this time under his complete control and for which he could take sole credit.

On 22 May 1928, Umberto Nobile and his crew set off from Spitzbergen in Norway on their aerial voyage to the North Pole in a brand new airship called, this time, the *Italia*. The outbound flight passed without a hitch, flying over the North Pole with ease before Nobile ordered the airship to turn around and head back to base. But on the return journey things began to go horribly wrong.

On 23 May, the airship began to lose altitude, eventually crashing on to the ice with a sickening thud. In the initial impact the nine members of the crew who were in the main cabin under the airship were thrown out on to the freezing Arctic ice. A tenth man, who was at the rear of the ship, was also thrown out by the impact but was killed as he hit the rock-hard icy surface.

Six crew members still remained on the airship, but as they stretched out their arms to help their fellow crewmen back on board the sudden movement caused the airship to lift off again, leaving the nine living crewmen and one dead one behind on the icy-cold surface near the North Pole. The men who remained on the airship may at first have thought themselves lucky, but fate took a hand and these men, and their airship, were never seen again.

But that still left nine very cold and frightened men out on the ice.

Amazingly, the crash had thrown not only men but supplies out on to the ice. A tent and a

57

radio survived the impact and the men were able to call for help. Armed with pots of red dye, which had also been thrown out by the impact, the men painted their tent bright red so that it could be seen from miles away and then waited to be rescued. What followed, however, was one fatal disaster after another.

The first radio message did not get through until 6 June, when it was picked up by a Russian radio operator. Roald Amundsen, who had led the first airship mission back in 1926, flew out to search for the men but he and his crew of four were killed on 18 June when their plane disappeared over the Arctic.

But after much searching, the men and their red tent were spotted on 20 June by an Italian pilot who was able to drop vital supplies to the men, who had been living on fish and the few meagre rations they had with them.

On 23 June, a Swedish pilot was able to land near the men and take their leader, Umberto Nobile, back to safety. Unfortunately, when the pilot returned for the rest of the men he too crashed and became trapped on the ice.

Finally, on 12 July 1928, seven weeks after the men had first crashed on to the ice, the remaining crew of the *Italia*, and the pilot who had crashed trying to rescue them, were picked up by a Russian ice-breaking ship called the *Krassin*.

This is a tragic story, made all the more so by the fact that every single death could have been avoided had Umberto Nobile been willing to share the credit for the first flight over the North Pole. Instead, his desire to claim all the credit for the mission saw him risk, and lose, the lives of twelve good men.

We all have to take risks from time to time. But if you are going to take a chance, make sure that it's in a good cause.

Umberto Nobile

CHAPTER THREE

Where can I find water?

JUNGLE

There are more bum-biting beasties in the jungle than anywhere else on Earth. In fact, it's fair to say that you'll be on the menu from the moment you arrive. Assuming you can get a moment's peace from the poisonous scorpions, flesh-eating plants, maneating tigers, tiger-eating snakes* and the truly impressive range of bugs capable of spreading slow, painful and miserable death with little more than a scratch, you might just find yourself in need of a drink.

Fortunately, jungles are very, very wet places – it's a bit like being in a huge, sweaty armpit. If you can't find a stream you can still get water from some of the many plants you'll see around you. Green bamboo, for example, contains lots of water. Grab hold of the top end of some bamboo shoots and bend them over before tying them to the ground. Cut the tops off the shoots and leave a bowl underneath to catch the water as it drips out overnight. In the morning you should have a bowlful of water – though it may get nicked by something bigger and nastier than you.

Banana trees are also a good source of water. Cut the tree down to within about 30 cm of the ground and then hollow out the stump to create a large bowl. Almost immediately, the roots of the tree will begin slowly filling the bowl with water. At first this water will be full of sap, which tastes even worse than Brussels sprouts.

CUT HERE

BANANA TREE

CUT OUT BOWL

GREEN BAMBOO

* OK, they don't eat tigers but you get the idea.

Throw this away, along with the next couple of refills. By about the fourth refill the water will taste much better. If you're really lucky the bowl will keep refilling for at least the next couple of days.

As with any water that you don't get from a tap or a bottle, be sure to boil it first to get rid of any germs as these can really put a downer on your day.

MOUNTAIN

They say that what goes up must come down, and that's especially true of water. Any rain water or melted snow will roll down the sides of a mountain and gather in puddles, pools, streams and, if you're really lucky, a lake stuffed full of fish. All you have to do is head downhill until you find a place where the water has collected.

You can even use animals as your guide – they always seem to know the best places to get a drink. If you follow their tracks they can often lead you to water. Birds also have a habit of hanging around near water, so take a look around and see if you can spot where they're gathering.

But be careful!

While cuddly fluffy sheep will be happy to share their water with you, wolves, bears and other beasties can be very selfish. You wouldn't want to end up as their lunch, so keep your eyes peeled for anything with bigger teeth than yours.

TOP TIP

Pigeons and doves are big drinkers and can only live near water. If you spot any hanging around you can be sure that there will be water nearby.

63

Once you've found some water be sure to boil it before you take a drink. Although it may look clean and clear there's every chance that it may be hiding bugs or man-made pollution (wee, mostly).

ARCTIC AND ANTARCTIC

You'd think that finding water to drink in the Arctic or Antarctic would be simple, wouldn't you? There's snow and ice everywhere! Surely all you have to do is eat it and you'd soon stop feeling thirsty?

But there's a catch.

To melt the water, your body will have to use up lots and lots of the energy that would normally be used to keep you warm. Eating snow will cool your body down very quickly and before you know it you'll end up turning yourself into an ice cube – this is very much the wrong kind of 'cool'.

So, boil any ice and snow you collect and have a nice hot drink instead. Oh, and make sure you stay well clear of any yellow snow – those polar bears have no shame.

DID YOU KNOW?

A place doesn't have to be hot to be a desert, it just needs to be dry. The McMurdo Dry Valleys in Antarctica, where temperatures average −20 °C, make up the coldest desert in the world.

DESERT

Sandy deserts can be beautiful places but the best thing you can do is avoid them at all costs. Unless you've always lived near a desert, and really know your way around, you'd be very lucky to survive for much more than forty-eight hours on your own.

There's very little water to be found in the desert and even the flies will fight you for a few drops of moisture. During the daytime you'll get fried in oven-like temperatures – the Sahara Desert has been known to reach an incredible 58 °C on a good day. At night you will get far worse than teeth-chatteringly cold – winter temperatures in the Gobi Desert, Central Asia, can drop below −20 °C after dark.

All of this is nature's way of telling you to go home.

Some desert tribes, such as the magnificent Bedouin, have found ways of surviving in these incredibly hostile conditions. They know exactly where all the wells are and just how much water they'll need to get from one to another. But you would have to be luckier than a lottery winner to find one of these wells by accident. Your best bet for survival in the Sahara, Western Desert, Sinai or the Arabian Desert is to keep an eye out for the Bedouin. They are good people who will be happy to save your life in an emergency.

But if you do find yourself stranded without water, look out for half-buried stones. Just before the sun rises on another beautiful day, turn the cool stones over and wait for dew to form on their surface. Licking this precious moisture off the stones might just keep you alive until rescue arrives. You may also find dew collecting on desert grass at this time of the day. It can be mopped up with a cloth and then squeezed out into your mouth.

WHY IS WATER SO IMPORTANT?

You're really just a big bag of water. Seriously! Over 70% of your body is made up of water, and if you don't keep this topped up then all sorts of horrible things will start to happen to you.

Don't believe me? Well, just for starters here are a few of the things you can expect if you don't drink enough water:

- Dry mouth
- Headaches
- Chapped or dry lips
- Dizziness
- Tiredness
- Loss of appetite

These may not sound too nasty, and they're not. But they are your body's way of telling you that something is wrong. The moment you pick up any of these clues you should drink some water straight away. If you don't, then the following things will start to happen:

- Confusion
- Dry, stinging eyes
- Loose skin
- A burning feeling in your stomach

TOP TIP

Even really filthy water can have its uses. To cut down on the amount of moisture you will lose by sweating, soak your clothing in this water and place a wet cloth or T-shirt over your head and around the back of your neck. This acts as a sun block and slows down water loss caused by sweating.

Sounds bad? It could be worse. Our final list of symptoms contains just one entry:

DEATH

Even if you learn nothing else from this book, you must remember that the most important thing you will need in a survival situation is water. Unless you're caught out in a hurricane or a blizzard, or a mountain lion is about to bite your bottom, everything else can wait.

HOW MUCH WATER WILL I NEED?

The amount of water you'll need to drink each day depends on where you are and what you're doing. In the temperate zones – places like northern Europe and the northern United States of America – you will need to drink about two litres of water a day. (The temperate zones are those bits of our beautiful planet that lie between the two Poles but well away from the equator.)

In much warmer countries, such as those you'd find along the equator – or even in parts of southern Europe during the summer – you'll have to drink much more water. The exact amount will depend on how much time you spend out in the sunshine and also on how active you are. For example, a really hardworking bricklayer in the Middle East might get through eight litres of water in a day – that's almost a bathful in a week!

THE 'WEE' TEST

One of the easiest ways of finding out whether or not you've drunk enough water is the 'wee test'. Next time you go for a wee take a look at the colour. Ideally, it should be a very pale greenish-yellow, completely see-through and have almost no smell (when fresh). Anything darker than this and you really should drink some water.

Remember: pale and clear, nothing to fear.

Wee, or 'urine' to give it the correct name, drains out of your body, taking with it many of the things you either don't need or which, if left to build up too much, might cause serious harm to your liver.

It's usually made up of a mixture of water and chemicals, such as ammonia (the smelly bit), and is a really important part of the process your body uses to keep the right balance of fluids and minerals.

TOP TIP

If your tent is any good it will, of course, be waterproof. This means that any water that lands on it will run off down the sides and end up on the ground. But rather than waste this run-off water, arrange the outer layer of your tent so that the rain-water can collect in troughs at the bottom of the tent. In the morning, transfer this pure rainwater into a bottle and you will have a source of clean water for the day.

DID YOU KNOW?

The chemicals used to make some fizzy drinks taste sweet travel straight through your body and are passed out the other end, unchanged, when you go for a wee.

Building a solar still

Build a solar still to get pure drinking water from the ground, from dirty water and even from mashed-up plants.

You will need:

- A hole in the ground
- A large sheet of clear plastic
- A few rocks
- A pebble or coin
- A water collector (a cup will be ideal)

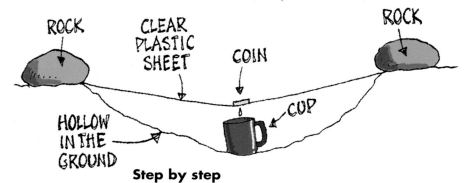

ROCK · CLEAR PLASTIC SHEET · COIN · ROCK · CUP · HOLLOW IN THE GROUND

Step by step

1. Clear a small hole in the ground.
2. Place the water collector in the centre of the bottom of the hole.
3. Cover the hole with a large, clear plastic sheet.
4. Secure the plastic sheet by placing rocks and pebbles around the edge of the hole (try to make sure that no air can escape from the hole).
5. Place a coin or small pebble on the plastic sheet directly above the water collector so that any water gathering on the underside of the plastic sheet will eventually drip into the water collector.
6. Sit back and wait for the sun to do its work.

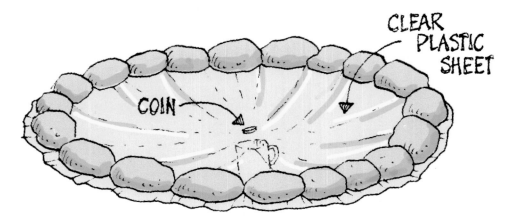

COIN

CLEAR PLASTIC SHEET

Why it works

The solar still is a really clever device for gathering and – most importantly – purifying water. Although it works by harnessing energy from the sun, which has been around since the birth of our solar system, the solar still is considered to be a fairly modern invention, not least because it relies on the use of a large sheet of clear plastic (which wasn't around until recently).

By building a solar still you'll be creating a mini greenhouse, trapping water vapour that would rise naturally from the ground in the hope that it will condense and cool on the inside of the plastic sheet before dripping down into a water collector. And best of all, the hotter things get, the better the solar still works.

You can use this device to purify dirty water too – even urine – simply by leaving it in a separate container underneath the plastic sheet. It can also be used to extract drinking water from mashed-up plants. As with dirty water, they are simply left under the plastic sheeting and any water they contain will to evaporate before gathering on the underside of the plastic sheet and then dripping into the water collector.

Make a water filter from natural materials

This is a very simple water filter that can be surprisingly effective at clearing much of the dirt out of water. This version is built inside a hollowed-out branch but you could, just as easily, use the sleeve from a waterproof jacket or the leg of a pair of waterproof trousers – so long as you don't need them for your own protection.

You will need:

- A hollowed-out branch or similar-sized watertight tube
- Handfuls of clean grass and leaves
- Some sand
- Some charcoal
- A stone large enough to block one end of the tube
- A container to collect water

Step by step

1. Jam the stone into one end of the tube (it should be tight enough to hold everything in place yet still allow water to drip out).
2. Pack lots of grass and leaves (or an old T-shirt) on top of the stone.
3. Add a layer of tightly packed sand above that layer.
4. Add a layer of tightly packed charcoal above that.
5. Add a final layer of tightly packed sand.
6. Add the top layer of grass and leaves, all the while making

sure that the contents of the tube are as tightly packed as you can manage.

7. Pour unfiltered water into the top of your natural water filter, allowing the first few run-throughs to empty on to the ground (it improves the taste).

8. Collect clean water in the container at the bottom of the tube after it has passed through the filter.

9. Boil any water collected in this way to remove any water-borne bacteria.

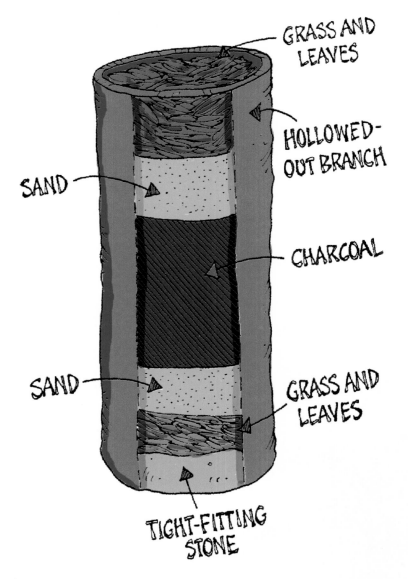

GRASS AND LEAVES

HOLLOWED-OUT BRANCH

SAND

CHARCOAL

SAND

GRASS AND LEAVES

TIGHT-FITTING STONE

Why it works

One of the vital bits of the posh water filter jugs that many of us have in our homes is nothing more than simple crushed charcoal. Charcoal is ordinary wood that has been burned until blackened and then ground up to make a surprisingly effective filter. You can find charcoal in the leftovers from a campfire.

Because the grains of charcoal are so fine, just about the only thing that can squeeze past them is water, which it does easily while leaving behind many of the nasty particulates that carry with them disease, death and sore bottoms.

Unfortunately, the germs that are carried in water cannot be filtered out in this way because they are truly tiny (yet often deadly) and so any water collected using this filter must still be boiled before it is drunk.

Survival Story

Water, water everywhere

Samoan fishermen Lapahele Sopi and Telea Pa'a survive for 132 days in an open boat.

When a group of Samoan fishermen set off for a day's fishing on a bright August morning in 2001 they could not possibly have imagined the nightmare that they were to face in their lightweight aluminium boat. Before their adventure was over, two of them would be dead and two more would be taken to the very edge of existence.

Yet it all started out so well. The four men were used to fishing the waters off the coast of their home island of Western Samoa and after a slow start the day's fishing began to pick up pace. Before long the boat was beginning to fill with fish, yet still the fishermen pulled more and more on board.

Soon the boat became so heavy with fish that it began to take on water. Realizing the mistake they had made, the men worked frantically, bailing out the water and cutting away the fishing lines that seemed to be trying to pull the boat under.

Yet still the boat continued to sink. Finally, in their desperation and with water pouring over the sides, they cut loose the two outboard motors which they had relied on to help them navigate the treacherous currents around Western Samoa. At last, the boat rose up in the water again.

Their lives had been saved for now, but at what price?

Without the powerful outboard motors the boat was entirely at the mercy of powerful and deadly sea currents and the men could only sit and watch as they drifted further and further away from land and out into the open ocean. Still, not to worry. Surely they would be picked up soon by one of the many other boats that fished around these waters?

But as the men soon discovered, a tiny boat is no match for a large ocean. In no time at all they were desperately in need of rescue. They launched distress flare after distress flare in an effort to call for help, yet try as they might they could not draw attention to themselves.

Imagine their frustration as the hours passed into days and the days into weeks, and still no sign of rescue. Imagine how they must have wished for an engine, or even a set of oars, as they passed tantalizingly close to islands and rocks - at one point they were so close to the Pacific island of Fiji that they could smell it, but still the currents drew them further and further away from any chance of rescue.

By now the situation in the boat had become truly desperate. The few supplies they had brought with them for the original day's fishing had long since run out. Most importantly, although completely surrounded by water, they had nothing to drink.

The men had no choice but to struggle on as best they could. When it rained they collected as much water as they could in the boat - it was to be their only source of fresh water.

For food they turned quite naturally to the sea. Despite having cut away their fishing lines the men were skilful enough to catch a few small fish. The occasional sea bird, pausing for a rest on the boat while crossing the ocean, was soon caught and killed and helped to add a little variety to the men's diet. But in the end it was the lack of water and their continued exposure to the weather that gradually wore them down. The first to die was also the oldest.

To'o Ioani was fifty-nine when he finally collapsed and died from the continued exposure, dehydration and malnutrition after one month adrift in the boat. In the cruel game that nature was playing with them, it was a case of one down, three to go.

Next to die was Tofi Lauvi, at forty-two the next oldest man in the boat. Eight weeks of poor diet and very little water were, literally, the death of him. After two long months in the boat the original team of four was down to just two. But still the ordeal was not over.

For the next two months the two surviving fishermen, Lapahele Sopi, thirty-six, and Telea Pa'a twenty-seven, continued to drift around the Pacific islands, floating close to land and firing off flares in the hope of rescue, but somehow always passing under the radar.

Finally, in November 2001, the men were spotted by a villager from Milne Bay, Papua New Guinea, who paddled out to meet them in his canoe after catching a glimpse of the very last of their flares. The two survivors were taken to Alotau Hospital in eastern Papua New Guinea, where they were treated by Dr Barry Kirby.

'It is a miracle they survived. They suffered from exposure and were basically on a starvation diet.' said Dr Kirby at the time. 'One man is unable to walk. He's very, very wasted and was probably a week away from death. The other man was quite strong considering his ordeal. The key to their survival was just determination and basically doing the right thing, not drinking too much salt water.'

Over the course of 132 days, the men had drifted 4,000 miles in their open boat. Of the original four, two had died.

one was close to death and the other was clearly a natural born survivor.

Those who survived did so because they were fairly young and very fit and had the sense not to drink sea water (it'll make you thirstier and then kill you).

If you ever found yourself in their position, what do you think your chances of survival would be?

CHAPTER FOUR

Food, glorious food

We need energy to do just about anything. And if you think of your body as a torch, then the food you eat provides the energy that makes the torch light up.

No food = no energy = no fun

The amount of energy you'll need depends on what you're up to. While doing everyday things like watching TV, playing in the park and reading books, a nine-year-old boy would have to eat food with an energy value of around 2,000 calories a day to stay at a normal weight. But in a survival situation, especially one that involved a long journey on foot over rough ground and in cold conditions, he would need lots more calories.

HOW MANY CALORIES DO I NEED?

Our age can have a big effect on the amount of food we need to eat. These are the number of calories you will need in a single day, depending on your age.

Age	Male	Female
1–3	1,250	1,200
4–6	1,700	1,550
7–10	2,000	1,800
11–14	2,220	1,850
15–18	2,800	2,100
Grown-ups	2,500	2,000

DID YOU KNOW?

There are more calories in a 50g bag of peanuts than there are in an average cheeseburger.

DID YOU KNOW?

A cyclist competing in a Tour de France mountain section will use up 10,000 calories in a single day.

WHERE CAN I FIND FOOD?

Look hard enough and you'll nearly always be able to find food. Anywhere that can support plenty of plants and wildlife can support you. You'll find fruit in the trees and growing on bushes. You may even find some vegetables, although they probably won't look like the kind of things that you might eat at the dinner table.

Generally speaking, **you should only eat foods you can recognize and which you know are safe to eat**. In this case, watching what other animals eat can be a guide, but you should be aware that they may have evolved ways of dealing with poisons that would kill you in an instant.

Talking of killing, if you're prepared to do it then you should be able to eat most small animals, birds and even insects, but be careful to stay away from anything with a poisonous sting or bite. If you're not prepared to kill your food, you can always steal its eggs – eggs are full of protein and are an excellent source of energy.

WHAT ABOUT THE DESERT?

Finding food in the desert is a different matter. In these regions you may, if you're very lucky, catch the odd reptile, insect or even a bird but your best bet for survival is to put all of your efforts into finding water and getting back to civilization as soon as possible. You can go for perhaps a couple of weeks without food but you'll be doing well to survive for more than a couple of days without water.

PLANTS YOU CAN EAT

The subject of wild foods is worth a book in itself, but here are a few things that you might find on your travels and which should be safe for you to eat so long as they haven't been sprayed with bug killer or weed killer.

As ever, if you're not sure then don't eat it.

Apples

Yes, apples. They grow on easy-to-climb trees and once ripe are easy to recognize. But some are very acidic, and should only be used for baking. Avoid these if you can, and never, ever steal apples from a tree growing in someone else's garden (unless you can run 400m in well under a minute).

Apple

Bananas

If you're in a hot country, you may be lucky enough to find these growing wild (they appear green when really fresh or not quite ripe). You'll probably have to climb up the banana tree to get them, but it's definitely worth the effort. Oh, and watch out for the big, hairy spiders who like to hide among the fruit.

Banana

Burdock root

Burdock

You can eat the root of the burdock plant. Gently pull it out of the ground, scrub it clean and slice it very thinly. Boil in water for about twenty minutes to get a potato-like vegetable dish. Don't eat the leaves, though, as these are all but impossible for humans to digest.

Blackberries

Blackberry

It's easy to find these in hedgerows in late summer. Don't forget to soak the blackberries briefly before you eat them as this will help to get rid of any nasty bugs that might be lurking in the fruit.

Cat-tail shoots

The cat-tail plant, which looks a little like a river bed reed, is found all over the world – it was a favourite of the Native Americans and is known as 'Cossack's Salad' in Russia. Peel the shoots and eat raw (they taste a little like cucumber). Alternatively, slice and stir-fry them or add to soup. Best eaten before the plant flowers in early summer.

Chicory

You can eat the leaves of the chicory plant after first boiling them to get rid of any bitterness. You can also roast, grind and make a coffee-like drink from the root. Chicory is an excellent source of minerals and vitamins A and C.

Chicory

Elder

The flowers of this plant can be cleaned and eaten raw, cooked or used to make tea. The berries are an excellent source of minerals and vitamin C.

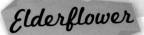

Elderflower

86

Garlic mustard

So called because it smells a little like garlic, this plant can be eaten raw or lightly boiled.

Gooseberries

Sour, sour, sour, but very good for you. The juicy ones tend to be a stripy lime green in colour and a little hairy.

Garlic Mustard

Gooseberries

Mulberries

Red (or purple) mulberries grow in tight clusters, as do the white Asian variety. The fruit can be eaten raw or cooked.

Mulberries

Nettles

Nettles

Wearing thick gloves to stop yourself getting stung, strip off the leaves and then steam or boil them (the leaves) before eating. The stems of young nettle plants can also be eaten after being prepared in the same way. Alternatively, nettle leaves can be dried and made into a tea.

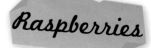

Raspberries

Like blackberries, they grow wild on bushes and resemble them in all but colour, being red when ripe but just as heavily stuffed with vitamin C. Fill your boots! (But not literally.)

Raspberries

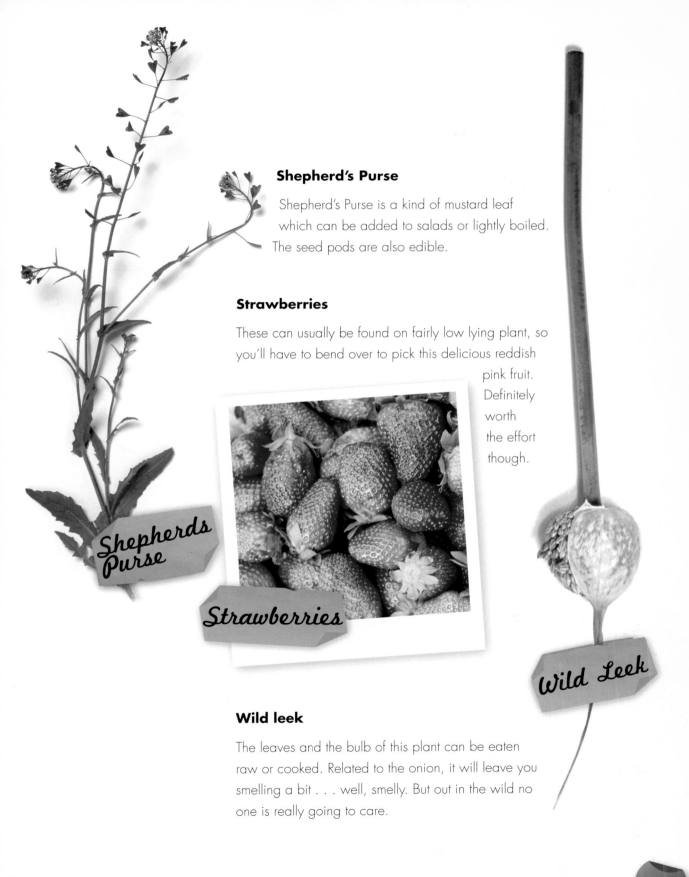

Shepherd's Purse

Shepherd's Purse is a kind of mustard leaf which can be added to salads or lightly boiled. The seed pods are also edible.

Strawberries

These can usually be found on fairly low lying plant, so you'll have to bend over to pick this delicious reddish pink fruit. Definitely worth the effort though.

Shepherds Purse

Strawberries

Wild Leek

Wild leek

The leaves and the bulb of this plant can be eaten raw or cooked. Related to the onion, it will leave you smelling a bit . . . well, smelly. But out in the wild no one is really going to care.

FISHING

Give a man a fish and he'll eat for a day; teach a man to fish and he'll eat for life. And why not? Fish is a wonderful source of low-fat protein which just sits and waits to be caught and eaten fresh (by far the best way to enjoy fish).

There is real skill involved in certain kinds of fishing, but in the battle for survival we simply don't have time to learn how to do this. Instead, we'll look at ways of catching fish that will allow you to concentrate on other things, like improving your shelter or foraging for fruit and vegetables.

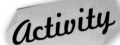

Activity

Catching fish with hooks and line

CARVED WOOD SHANKS

If you don't have any fishing hooks with you, you can always make them from wire, pins and needles or even thorns and bits of bone. Anything small enough to fit in the mouth of a fish will do, so long as it will stay in place after the bait has been taken. (Worms and maggots make excellent bait.)

Ideally, you should attach hooks to a number of short pieces of line and then attach these fish hook/line combinations to a single horizontal line which is then strung between two posts across a river. You can leave this in place all day and return later when, with any luck, several fish will have taken the bait and you will be having fish for dinner.

THORN HOOKS

CARVED WOOD GORGE HOOK

WIRE

Trapping fish

An alternative to using fish hooks and line, especially when you don't have access to either, is to build a trap of some sort. A very effective trap involves placing a 'basket' woven from thin branches into a river with the narrow entrance of the basket facing upstream (towards the direction from which the river is flowing).

BASKET FISH TRAP

Several fish may swim into the basket but very few will have the brains or the luck to find their way out again. Simply pull the basket up out of the water at the end of the day to pick up your catch.

If you don't want to go to the trouble of making a basket, you could instead make a 'pool' or 'shore' trap. This involves pushing branches into the river bed to create a three-sided fence through which water can pass but not fish. Add another two rows of branches to act as a funnel, which will drive the fish into the trap. When the time is right, block the entrance/exit to the trap and grab your fish supper. (This can be a lot harder than it sounds, but should keep you amused for a while.)

CURRENT

POOL OR SHORE FISH TRAP

KEEPING IT FRESH

Unless you're attempting to survive in very cold conditions, then the chances are that any food you gather or catch will very soon start to go off. It's not really possible to preserve food in the wild unless you really know what you're doing so often the best approach is to eat only fresh food.

If you are setting out on a big adventure you should bring lots of dried food with you. Rice and pasta last for ages and can be boiled up when needed. Dried fruit is also a very good source of energy and any serious outdoorsman will always carry a bag of raisins or dried apricots and bananas.

DID YOU KNOW?

Because the heat of the desert will turn food bad very quickly – and there really is nowhere to plug in a fridge – the Bedouin carry their food with them in the form of living animals. Sheep, goats and camels travel alongside them and are milked or slaughtered when needed. That way the milk is always fresh and the meat never goes off.

DID YOU KNOW?

When the warriors of Genghis Khan conquered most of the known world they did so on a diet of blood, which was drained in small amounts from their horses and then mixed with milk to make a very pink drink that was high in vitamins and minerals.

GENGHIS KHAN

THE IMPORTANCE OF COFFEE

If you ever meet the Bedouin you should never turn down their offer of a cup of coffee as it is part of an important ritual in their society. The first cup, called El-Heif, is tasted by the host to show that it is safe to drink. The second cup, called El-Keif, should be poured and drunk by you. The third cup, called El-Dheif, should also be drunk by you. When you have finished the third cup you should shake the dregs out and hand it back to your host. Once you have drunk coffee in this way you will, by Bedouin tradition, be placed under the protection of your host.

Making a cooking fire

The best kind of fire for cooking food is called a log cabin fire. Gather firewood and kindling, using only fallen branches.

DID YOU KNOW?

The heat from a cooking fire changes the chemical make-up of the food you eat. This change is what we are really talking about when we say that food has been cooked. But you can get the same effect using natural fruit acids. This allows you to 'cook' fresh salmon, for example, by soaking it for several hours in freshly squeezed lemon or lime juice.

①

Build your fire at least 3 metres away from tents and trees.

Start with a small pile
of kindling.

Construct a pyramid of
dry twigs and small sticks.
Put two logs side by side
roughly 30cm apart. Then
add two more logs at right
angles to the first two.
Keep building up the fire
in this way, adding kindling
as you go.

Light kindling.

Food can be 'roasted' in the
centre of the fire or cooked
in a tray or pan placed on the
top. The arrangement of the
logs means that oxygen will be
drawn into the bottom of the
fire and will heat to a cooking
temperature as it moves
rapidly through the stack.

WHAT DOES SQUIRREL TASTE LIKE?

Generally speaking, anything cat-sized or smaller tends to taste a bit like chicken, as do most birds once they've been cooked. Creatures that are roughly dog-sized will taste like pork but anything larger, such as an ostrich, has a taste and texture similar to beef.

96

TOP TIP FOR
EATING WORMS

Worms are a great source of protein, which is essential if you are going to last any time at all in the wild. If the thought of eating them raw turns your stomach, then try drying them out by the fire when you have killed them and adding them to whatever else you are cooking (along with a good pinch of chilli powder). You can also prepare grubs and centipedes in this way.

Activity

Making survival biscuits

These survival biscuits are easy to make in the kitchen at home and, on sunny days, can be cooked in a pizza-box (or solar) oven (see p.100).

You will need:

- 100g of butter
- 50g of soft brown sugar
- 4 tablespoons of golden syrup
- 250g rolled or porridge oats
- Some very finely chopped dried apricots
- A saucepan
- A mixing spoon
- A plate greased with butter

Step by step

1. Heat the butter, sugar and syrup in the saucepan over a low heat until the butter has melted and the sugar has dissolved.

2. Add the oats and the apricots to the mixture and stir well.

3. Spread the mixture thinly over the greased plate.

4. Put the plate in the solar oven and wait for the mixture to cook before cutting it into moist (and yummy) survival biscuits. Or you can bake these in a conventional oven on a metal baking sheet at 190 °C/375 °F/gas mark 5 for 15 minutes.

Why it works

The mixture of two forms of sugar (brown sugar and syrup), lots of fat (the butter) and fruit acids might be a bit much for your body to cope with every day. In fact, it would probably make you fat. But in the short term biscuits like these can provide the energy you need to survive an emergency and stay alive until help arrives. They also taste great.

Making a pizza-box oven

You can make yourself a solar oven (that's one that is powered by the sun) from a couple of old pizza boxes. Use this oven to bake your survival biscuits, but don't try to cook raw meat or fish using this method as the oven will probably not get hot enough to cook the food safely.

You will need:

- Two pizza boxes (one large, one small)
- A pencil
- A craft knife
- Some aluminium foil
- Some old newspaper
- A pot of non-toxic black paint
- A paint brush
- Some glue
- Some sticky tape
- A plate
- Some clear plastic or clingfilm

Step by step

1. Place the smaller pizza box centrally on top of the large pizza box and draw round it.

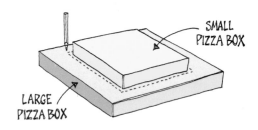

SMALL PIZZA BOX

LARGE PIZZA BOX

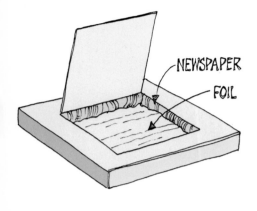

NEWSPAPER

FOIL

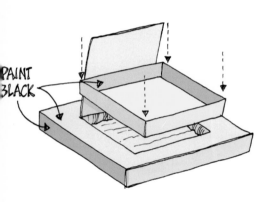

PAINT BLACK

FOIL

SUNLIGHT

CLEAR PLASTIC

FOOD

2. Cut along three side of the square you have just drawn but leave the fourth side attached to form a lid.

3. Line the inside of the large box with aluminium foil, then stuff newspaper around the edges of the box. (This will act as insulation for your oven, helping to hold in any heat.)

4. Remove and discard the lid of the small box and fit what's left into the middle of the large box, adding extra newspaper as needed to fill any remaining space between the two boxes.

5. Paint the inside of the small box and the whole of the outside of the large box with black paint. Glue aluminium foil to the inside of the lid.

6. Place the food you'd like to cook on a plate and put it into the oven before covering the opening of the oven with clear plastic or wrapping it in clingfilm. This will trap the energy coming from the sun.

7. Line up your pizza-box oven so that the sun's rays are reflected on to the food by the foil-lined lid.

8. Sit back and wait for the sun to do what it does best.

Why it works

Almost everything on Earth gets its energy from the sun. Energy is transferred to us via the sun's rays where it is absorbed by plants, which are eaten by animals which are then, along with the plants, eaten by us. This energy can also be trapped in a greenhouse and used to help plants grow in climates that might not normally suit them. In much the same way, energy can be trapped and used to cook food, in this case survival biscuits.

Survival Story: Feeling hungry?

They survived for ten weeks on a mountain top without supplies. So what did they find to eat?

A routine flight between the South American countries of Uruguay and Chile took off without incident on Friday 13 October 1972. Some might say that Friday the 13th is a bad day to fly, but this didn't seem to bother anyone on the plane. Unfortunately, whether or not anyone was superstitious didn't seem to matter. Luck was definitely not on their side that day.

The plane disappeared while passing over the Andes mountain range, one of the last remaining wildernesses on Earth. Severe weather conditions hampered any rescue attempts and, try as they might, the search parties could find no trace of the plane and its passengers. Tragically, this was because they were looking in the wrong place.

The plane had indeed come down, killing twenty passengers and crew, but on the morning of 14 October it soon became obvious to the survivors that the plane was nowhere near its last reported position, having been blown off course by a strong headwind.

Realizing that it might be some time before they were rescued, the remaining passengers began to sift through the wreckage of the plane, converting parts of it into a shelter and gathering food (mostly chocolate bars and crisps) from among the luggage they found.

On the eighth day an electronics student who had been on board the plane managed to get a simple transistor radio working just in time to hear that the search for the missing plane had been abandoned. Things were now getting desperate, but they were about to get a whole lot worse.

Six days later tragedy struck again when an avalanche killed a further eight survivors and buried most of the wreckage of the plane, making it entirely invisible from the air. To add to their frustration, the survivors had to watch from the ground as passing aircraft, which might have spotted the wreckage of their plane, flew straight by, unable to pick out their snow-buried aircraft from among the rocky outcrops near the top of the mountain.

With little food left and even less chance of rescue, the remaining survivors had some hard choices to make. If they didn't find food soon they would all die on this mountainside. And the only possible source of nourishment lay buried in the makeshift cemetery that they had dug near the wreckage.

With a heavy heart one of the survivors bowed to the inevitable and grabbed a piece of broken glass. Reluctantly, he began to cut strips of flesh from the dead bodies, forcing it down his throat as he went along. Gradually the others joined him.

As their bodies grew stronger on the flesh of their dead fellow travellers, the survivors began to turn their attention to getting down off the mountain. After sixty-two days in the snow, the two strongest men in the team headed west across the mountain range in search of rescue.

Finally, after ten days' hard walking, they found civilization and were able to call for help. On 22 December, over two months after the plane had crashed into the mountain, the two men returned with helicopters from the Chilean Air Force to lift the remaining fourteen survivors to safety.

It wasn't until the survivors were finally down off the mountain that people began to question how they had managed to keep themselves alive for so long in such incredibly harsh conditions. What had happened to the rest of

the passengers and crew? What had the survivors found to eat? And why were some of them in such apparently good health?

Four days after the rescue a newspaper in Chile became the first to break the news that the survivors had eaten the dead. Two days later, at a press conference, the remaining passengers finally admitted the truth.

No matter what you feel about eating human flesh, it would be wrong to judge these survivors by the standards of ordinary life. These people were not savages. Many were highly educated people who simply did what they had to do in order to live for another day in the hope that rescue would come.

What would you have done in their position? Could you have chosen to starve to death in the snow rather than eat the person who had been travelling in the next seat to you? With any luck you will never have to make that choice.

CHAPTER FIVE

Working together, staying in touch

The key to survival in any dangerous situation is to work closely with those around you – assuming you're lucky enough not to be lost on your own. You can support each other when things are looking bad, find the courage to do things that might normally frighten you if you were on your own, and share any food and drink you have – although there can be all kinds of punch-ups if someone eats the last chocolate biscuit.

If you have a friend with you then one of you can get the fire going while the other hunts for food. You can also work together to build a shelter and keep each other company when the nights get dark and cold and scary and, best of all, you'll have someone to back up your amazing story when you finally get home and tell your friends about the adventure you've been on.

SMOKE SIGNALS

You can often use the things around you to call for help. For example, if you've managed to get a fire going then you already have a great source of signal power. The smoke from your fire will be visible for miles around, but while this may draw attention there is nothing about the smoke that will make it any different from an ordinary, small camp fire.

As far as anyone else knows, you might be frying up a bit of bacon for breakfast rather than entering your fourth day in lost-in-the-mountains hell.

This is the time to make a like a Native American and start sending smoke signals. You needn't be descended from the Apache to be able to do this. After all, most of the people who will 'read' your smoke probably don't know traditional Native American smoke signals from a chip-pan fire.

They will, however, notice the difference between ordinary smoke from a camp fire and smoke that seems to be sending a signal. All you need do is use a blanket to cover the fire briefly and at intervals so that the smoke rises from the fire in bursts rather than as a continuous stream. If you get really good at this you might be able to send an SOS message, but irregular smoke may well be enough to attract the attention of the rescue team.

DID YOU KNOW?

SETI, the Search for Extraterrestrial Intelligence, scans the stars for signs of alien intelligence. In among the background noise left over from the Big Bang at the start of the universe, they are searching for a signal that can only have been made artificially. Just as there are no straight lines in nature, so there are no randomly occurring regular signals, or pulses, from space. The exception to this rule was found with the discovery of pulsars (pulsating stars) by the astronomer Jocelyn Bell Burnell in 1967. At first sight these seemed to be sending a regular signal from space. They looked so much like signals from another world that she wrote the letters 'LGM' next to a print-out of the signal, in the belief that it might possibly have been sent by 'Little Green Men'.

MORSE CODE

Morse code has been used for well over a hundred years to send messages between people who were unable, for whatever reason, to talk to each other. While the number of people who can 'read' Morse code is in decline, any rescue team and very many of your fellow adventurers will be able to recognise an SOS or call for help when they see or hear one.

Morse code substitutes short dots and long dashes for the letters of the alphabet. This means that messages can be sent using light, sound, smoke or just about anything else that can represent a dot or a dash.

For example, the letter S in Morse code is represented as three dots, like this: ● ● ●

The letter O in Morse code is represented by three dashes, like this: – – –

Put them together and you can create the simple distress signal, recognizable the world over, of SOS: ● ● ● – – – ● ● ●
or dot/dot/dot   dash/dash/dash   dot/dot/dot.

A	● –	B	– ● ● ●	C	– ● – ●
D	– ● ●	E	●	F	● ● – ●
G	– – ●	H	● ● ● ●	I	● ●
J	● – – –	K	– ● –	L	● – ● ●
M	– –	N	– ●	O	– – –
P	● – – ●	Q	– – ● –	R	● – ●
S	● ● ●	T	–	U	● ● –
V	● ● ● –	W	● – –	X	– ● ● –
Y	– ● – –	Z	– – ● ●		

GROOVY, BABY

Morse code has a rhythm, or groove, all of its own. Each dot or dash that makes up a letter counts as a single beat. The space between each letter should be filled with a pause lasting for one of these beats and the spaces between sentences are generally seven beats long – that way anyone listening in can be certain that your sentence has finished.

DID YOU KNOW?

The international SOS was first adopted by Germany in 1905 and caught on very soon afterwards. In English, the SOS is said to stand for 'Save Our Souls', but this was probably just an easy way for English-speaking people to remember the sequence of letters.

DID YOU KNOW?

Samuel Finley Breese Morse (1791–1872), or 'Sam' to his mum, was an American painter who, with Alfred Vail, invented the Morse code – bet you can tell who was the pushier person in that partnership. Morse code is based closely on a code created for an earlier telegraph system.

DID YOU KNOW?

In the daytime you can use a mirror to signal for help by reflecting sunlight. This works just like a torch (only much brighter). Even if you don't have a mirror with you it is still possible to use the sun to signal for help, by using a similarly reflective surface, such as a CD or even a foil wrapper.

YOU'RE THE BOSS!

In a survival situation, as the only person who has made adequate preparation (well, you're reading this book, aren't you?), you might be called on to lead a group to safety. Being a group leader can be a scary task, especially if you haven't done it before. But there are some things you can do to make sure that you are a good and effective group leader – rather than the kind who gets left behind at the bottom of a large cliff.

Be full of enthusiasm

If you're not up for the task then how can you expect anyone else to be?

Stay cool

Don't try to dominate the group. If you're talking sense and convincing people that you know the best way to survive then they will follow you. Most importantly, try to keep your sense of humour at all times. If you can laugh at a problem you can make that problem smaller.

Don't judge

Everyone makes mistakes. Even you! Try not to judge people on their mistakes. If you must judge, then judge them on their effort.

Be positive

Plan for the worst, but assume the best. You almost certainly will be rescued and when you are you'll have a great story to tell. As a wise man once said: 'One day this will be twenty years from now.'

Be flexible

You may have made a plan, but you might have to change it. Heading in one direction, even when you suspect it is the wrong one, simply because you told the group that you would, is a great way of ending up dead. Don't die of stupidity – there are already enough volunteers for this.

Know yourself and your group

Figure out what everyone, including yourself, is capable of and work within these limits.

Share

Groups are always stronger than individuals. By sharing everything fairly, be it work, food or ideas, then the group can only get stronger.

BLACK BEAR

OTTER

RED FOX

BOBCAT

WOLF

MOOSE

Animal trackers

This is a really great game to play with a group of friends. Each person should use a piece of card to create a stencil of their favourite animal tracks, such as a bear, lion or wolf. Try to make them life-sized.

Cut lots of each set of prints out of paper or card.

Once you've finished making your animal tracks, one of you must be appointed as the tracker. The tracker then waits for three minutes while the others each leave a trail their special animal tracks. These tracks should be the only clues they leave on the way to their hiding places.

After three minutes the tracker goes to work, searching for the tracks and, with any luck, following them to the hiding places each 'animal' has chosen.

When successfully tracked down, each 'animal' turns into a tracker, helping the original tracker to find the others in the game until everyone is found and the game can begin again, this time with a new tracker.

Treasure Hunt

Create a treasure map that your friends can follow. Try not to make it too easy as this will mean that the game will be over in no time, but don't make it so difficult that only an expert in cryptic crosswords can solve it.

You could try to incorporate some of the things you have learned from this book into your treasure hunt. For example, rather than give out a full map, you could use compass directions to make the game more interesting. This might involve a set of instructions such as 'Head to the farm gate and then travel due north for twenty paces, then west for ten more to find the next clue.' Clues can be scattered along the trail for your friends to find.

You could even build other elements into the game, such as signalling. For example, you could write 'Travel east from the old oak tree for ten paces then turn south and send a greeting signal directly ahead and wait for the reply and next set of instructions.' You should then lie in wait before sending a signal such as 'East ten paces, then due north to next clue.'

Walk 25 paces north –
Turn right at old tree –
Walk east for 10 paces –
Over the footbridge –
Turn left –
Walk 30 paces north-east –
Turn left at the fence –
After 20 paces turn south –
Walk 25 paces –
Look between the two tall trees –

CALLING FOR HELP WHILE AT SEA

Sailors are trained to recognize certain distress signals and will always come to your aid if they pick up your call for help. There are a number of ways of calling for help while at sea:

1. If you have a radio, you can send a 'Mayday' message on the VHF radio channel 16 (156.8 MHz) or, if using a High Frequency transmitter, on 2182 kHz. ('Mayday' probably comes from the French 'm'aidez', meaning 'help me'.)

2. Send an SOS Morse code message using a torch or a radio.

3. Fire off an orange smoke flare.

4. Slowly raise and lower your outstretched arms by your sides (as if making snow angels or trying to fly).

5. Fly your flag upside down. This works fine with the Stars and Stripes, as almost the whole world has seen this flag and will recognize that it is upside down. But even most British people would be unable to recognize that their national flag was flying upside down. In this case, tie a knot in it.

CALLING FOR HELP WHILE IN AN AEROPLANE

Distress signals while in flight are used to let air traffic control know that there is a problem. Once alerted, they will then transmit your last known position, as indicated by the distress signal, to rescuers on the ground. While on a civilian aircraft transmit your call for help on the 121.5 MHz frequency. If on a military aircraft use the 243 MHz frequency.

If your radio isn't working, it's still possible to signal that you are in distress by flying in a triangular pattern, making a series of 120 ° turns for the corners of the triangle.

CALLING FOR HELP WHILE UP A MOUNTAIN

If you think that a mountain rescue team are close by, you can call for help by using a whistle or torch. In many countries this involves no more than blowing six sharp blasts on your whistle and then repeating this pattern at one-minute intervals. Alternatively, you can send six flashes of light with the aid of a torch, again at one-minute intervals.

You will know that your distress signal has been picked up when mountain rescue replies to you with three blasts. Continue to repeat the signal until you are found.

LEAVING TRACKS

There are many different organizations that use tracking signals to leave messages for friends and to act as a warning for anyone else who may come along (and who knows how to read the signals).

Here are a number of commonly used signs as used by the scouts and other similar organizations.

A simple arrow made from twigs or stones means 'Walk this way'.

An 'X' on the ground means 'Danger, do not walk this way'. (You might get eaten or fall down a hidden mineshaft.)

Just like ordinary street signs, this arrow can indicate 'Turn right' or 'Turn left', depending on which direction it points.

This arrangement of sticks, combined with an arrow, is used to indicate where water can be found.

These two twigs (which look like the pause sign on a DVD remote control) are combined with an arrow to show that there is an obstacle lying in the direction of the arrow. This might be a rock-fall or perhaps a fallen tree.

This clever arrangement of twigs shows that the group has split into two smaller groups, with two people following the route indicated by one arrow and four people following the route indicated by the other arrow.

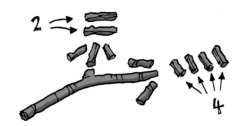

4

This message tells whoever finds it that there is another, possibly more important, message hidden further along the route in the direction of the arrow. The number of rows or number of stones within the box shape indicates the number of ordinary steps that need to be taken before the message is reached.

A full stop in a circle tells whoever is following your trail that you have finished and have either gone home or headed back to camp. It is the survivalist's equivalent of writing 'Game over'.

CHAPTER SIX

The Ultimate Survival Kit

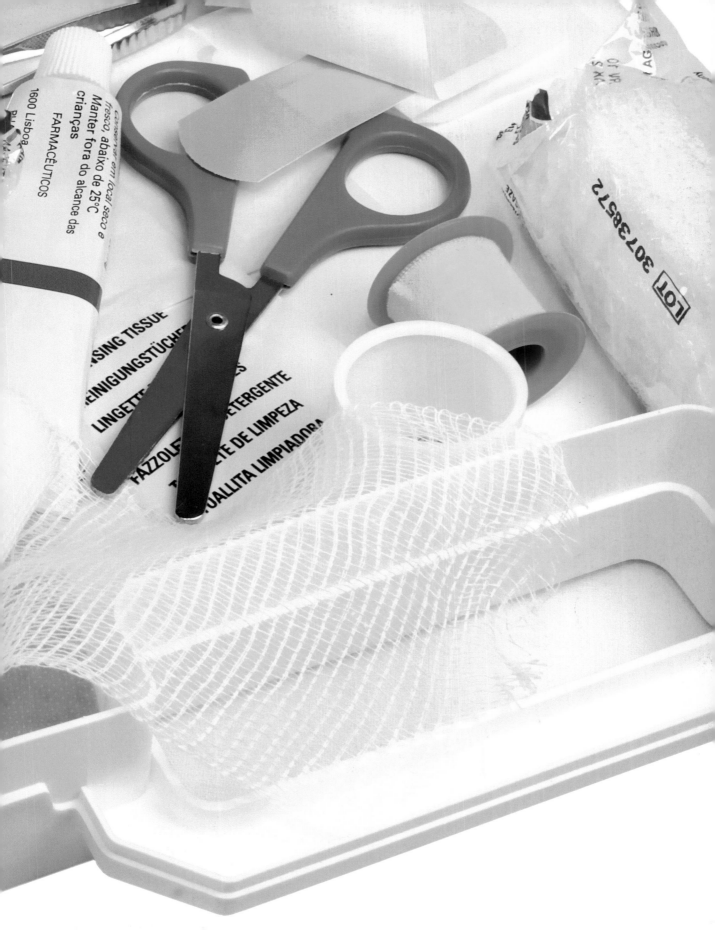

There's no such thing as bad weather. There's only unsuitable clothing and poor preparation. Properly clothed, equipped and trained, you should be able to survive – and thrive – just about anywhere in the world.

Key to your survival will be a good, well-thought-out survival kit. This will contain everything you'll need to survive in both the short and long term in any just about any situation and should always be taken when you are setting out on an adventure.

Some people also like to have a mini survival kit. This is a much reduced version of the main survival kit and is usually carried at all times by those who like to feel prepared. This may seem a little over the top, but you wouldn't set off on a long car journey without carrying at least a spare wheel and the number of a breakdown service, so why head off into the cold, cruel world without the very basics of survival?

WHAT SHOULD WE CARRY?

Here's a suggested mini survival kit for you. Perhaps not everything here will be quite right for the climate you are likely to find yourself in, so adapt as you see fit. But always bear in mind the key things you will need to survive in any life-threatening situation – water, shelter, fire, food – and make sure you include them in your planning.

Bin bags

Map

Spare batteries

Mirror

Compass

Magnifying glass

First-aid kit

Clear plastic

Survival blanket

Gaffer tape

Wet wipes

Cooking tin

Compass

Oh, come on! You know what a compass is for by now. Don't leave home without one.

Map

Didn't bring a map? You'll be telling us you forgot your compass next.

Magnifying glass

Not only can this be used to pick up tiny details on a map, the magnifying glass can also be used to start a fire by concentrating energy from the sun on to a small spot of dry tinder, which will eventually heat up and burst into flames so long as the sun is bright enough.

Pencil and several sheets of blank paper

What better way to leave a note for your rescuers than to use a pencil and paper? You can also use this to keep a diary, sketch your surroundings when bored and, if necessary, start a fire. The added bonus with a pencil is that it doesn't suddenly run out of ink and, unlike most pens, will always write in sub-zero temperatures.

DID YOU KNOW?

The tragic yet fascinating diaries kept by Captain Scott on his ill-fated journey to the South Pole in 1911 were recovered and were found to have been written in pencil, the reason being that the ink in a pen would have frozen and been useless in the sub-zero temperatures that ultimately killed the captain and his team.

Fishing line and hooks

Take a good length of fishing line (you can always cut it down to size) and some hooks. Use strong line and simply tie the hooks to the line and leave baited while you go off and get on with the business of survival. If all goes well, you should have a fish supper waiting for you when you return later.

Mirror

A mirror can be used to send signals to a rescuer or to re-focus the rays of the sun in order to help start a fire.

A whistle

This needn't be anything fancy, just so long as it makes a very loud noise. This can be used to summon help, send signals and, at a push, frighten away wild animals. The real advantage of this piece of equipment is that the batteries never run out and it needs no replacement parts.

LED torch

These torches are the new kids on the block, replacing the good but not so bright conventional battery and bulb torch. Light-emitting diodes (the LED bit) are powered by tiny, flat batteries which weigh little, are easy to store and, in combination with the LEDs, produce a very bright and consistent light which is great for signalling or simply finding your way around after dark. Choose one with a white light – they are available in a range of colours with red being the least bright.

Spare batteries

It's often a good idea to tape at least one set of spare batteries to anything that needs them (such as your torch) and keep an additional set in your kit. That way you'll always have a spare set to hand, even if you lose the rest of your survival kit.

Gaffer tape (aka duct tape)

If you can find a place for a roll of gaffer tape you won't regret it. This stuff can be used to hold together shelters and clothing, to replace sticking plasters (but don't forget to include a dressing) and to waterproof small items. Take it – you'll be sure to find a use for it.

Survival blanket

The survival blanket is a relatively modern piece of equipment and one that we are all familiar with as they are a very noticeable addition to disaster scenes on the news and racing events on TV. These lengths of man-made silvery material reflect your own body heat straight back at you, helping to keep you warm. Wear it like a shawl – never under your other clothes or right next to your skin (or you'll end up in a cold, damp puddle of your own sweat).

They can also make a great sun block and even be used as a signalling mirror. They're waterproof, weigh next to nothing and take up very little space, so there really is no reason for you not to have one in your survival kit.

Large sheet of clear plastic

Go to a builders' supplies store or a garden centre and buy the largest sheet of clear plastic you can carry in your kit. This one sheet can have many vital uses, including shelter, weatherproofing and providing water, either as part of a solar still or as a means of catching rainwater or river water. You can even keep fish in it! This inexpensive item more than justifies its presence in the kit.

Large bin bags

You can't have too many of these, especially in damp conditions. They can be adapted to make over-shoes, ponchos or even a mini shelter. Not bad for a rubbish bag.

Wet wipes

It's a wash in bag, and very welcome too. They also come in very handy for wiping your bum, making them arguably one of the finest achievements of humanity.

Resealable freezer bags

The uses of these bags are only limited by our imaginations. Food storage, waterproofing, makeshift water bottle . . . the list is endless. But only if you bring the resealable kind.

Small cooking tin

How else are you going to cook your food, boil your water, make your morning coffee, etc? Sometimes these can be bought in sets of three – useful if you have guests around the camp fire.

A selection of herbs and spices

Nothing improves the taste of a worm like a pinch of chilli powder. Use enough and just about anything is edible, which is probably just as well. Add a little salt and pepper for additional flavouring.

Boiled sweets and some biscuits

Strictly for use in desperate and dangerous survival situations (unless there's ages to go until lunchtime), boiled sweets and biscuits can supply a quick burst of energy when needed. Bananas and dried apricots can also do this and are much better for you, but where's the fun in that?

£20 note

There's not much point escaping from the wilderness only to discover that you can't pay for basic services when you get back to civilization. After all, imagine stumbling across a roadside cafe after four days lost in the woods only to find that you can't order double egg, chips and beans because you don't have any money. A large bank note is easy to conceal, takes up almost no space and buys an awful lot of chips, so you might as well take one.

SURVIVAL QUIZ

Chapter 1

Q. I live in a square house with four walls, each of which has a window. But every one of my windows faces south. Where do I live?

A. The North Pole

B. The South Pole

C. Chelmsford

Q. Why don't polar bears eat penguins?

A. They don't like the taste

B. They live on opposite sides of the world from each other

C. They prefer a good curry

Q. You should always let someone know where you're going because . . .

A. People are nosey

B. That way someone will know where to look for you if you don't come home

C. That way they'll miss you when you're gone

Chapter 2

Q. How can I avoid heatstroke?

A. By eating lots of ice cream

B. By wearing loose-fitting, cool clothing and drinking lots of water

C. I'm, like, too cool for heatstroke

Q. What is a safe temperature for human beings?

A. 98.6 °C

B. 38 °C

C. That's a good question

Q. Sleeping in horse manure is a good idea because . . .

A. It probably smells better than you do

B. The heat given off by the decomposing manure will keep you warm and save your life

C. It will leave your skin feeling fresh and tingling

Chapter 3

Q. Why should you avoid deserts if you have ginger hair and freckles?

A. The colour of the sand will clash with the colour of your hair

B. You'll burn and peel

C. You're far too cool to be seen in a desert

Q. You should include charcoal in your water filter because . . .

A. You can also use it to draw pictures while the water is filtering

B. Its fine grains mean that it will stop most impurities from passing through the filter

C. It's a good way of using up charcoal

Q. The most important thing you can do in any survival situation is . . .

A. Panic

B. Find water

C. Find water and then panic

Chapter 4

Q. Squirrel meat tastes a lot like . . .

A. Chicken nuggets

B. Fish and chips

C. My dog Rover

Q. How many calories should a boy aged 7–10 eat in a day?

A. 200

B. 2,000

C. 20,000

Q. Worms and maggots make very good . . .

A. Soup

B. Fishing bait

C. Furniture

Chapter 5

Q. In English, SOS stands for . . .

A. Save our sausages

B. Save our souls

C. Save our socks

Q. Flying your flag upside down tells everyone that . . .

A. You were not quite awake this morning

B. You're a bit of a rebel and you don't care who knows it

C. You need help

Q. Six blasts on a whistle suggest that . . .

A. It's party time, baby!

B. The game is over

C. You need to be rescued

Chapter 6

Q. You should never go on a big adventure without taking . . .

A. Clean underpants

B. Your Ultimate Survival Kit

C. Your mum

Q. Wet wipes are among the finest achievements of humanity because . . .

A. They are both elegant and fragrant

B. Girls like the way they smell

C. They're great for wiping your bum

INDEX

A-frame fire 52
agal 43
air ambulance 35
air conditioning 39
air traffic control 117
Amundsen, Roald 56, 58
animals
    fur 48, 49
    skins 48
    taste of cooked 96
    trackers 114
Antarctic 64
apples 84
Arabian Desert 65
Arctic 57, 58, 64

banana tree 62–3
bananas 85, 131
bank note 131
batteries, spare 128
Beaufort scale 26
Bedouin 16, 43, 55, 65, 92, 93
bees, desert 66
Big Dipper (the Plough) 17
bin bags, large 129
birds 63, 77, 96
biscuits 131
    survival 98–9, 101
bivouac bags 55
blackberries 85
blanket, survival 129
blood circulation 39, 45
body heat 5, 47
boots 4, 41, 44, 47, 49

bourque 43
burdock root 85
Burnell, Jocelyn Bell 109

calories 82–3
cannibalism 102–5
cat-tail shoots 86
caves 54
charcoal 74
chicory 86
CIA 5
clothing 124
    Arctic 48–9
    be prepared 5, 33
    Bedouin 43
    damp 45
    hats 5, 6, 39, 41
    lightweight 41, 44
    warm 39, 47
coffee 93
compass 13–15, 16, 18, 21,
    24, 126
    sun 28, 29
    wristwatch as a 30–31
contour lines 19
cooking tin 130

dehydration 40
    death due to 67, 77, 79
    symptoms of 66–7
desert
    the coldest 64
    navigation 16
    shelter 55
    temperatures 65
    water in 65–6
    wells 65

distress flares 76, 77, 78, 116
distress signals
    aeroplane 117
    mountain 118
    sea 116
dogs, sled 49
dried fruit 92, 131
drinks
    drinking water see water,
        drinking
    fizzy 69
    and heatstroke 42
    hot 39, 47, 64

Earth
    magnetic field 15
    rotation of 15, 17, 31
elderberry 86
electrolytes 69
emergency services 42, 52
energy 82, 83, 92, 101, 131
equator 22

fire
    A-frame 52
    cooking 94–5
    making a 39, 47, 50, 126,
        127
    putting out 53
    signal 7
    smoke signals 108–9
    tepee 51
firelighters 50
fishing 75, 77
    hooks and line 90, 127
    trapping fish 91
fitness 4

flag-flying, upside down 116
flashlight 118, 128
fleece top/trousers 48
following a heading 21–2
food
    calories needed 82–3
    dried 92, 131
    fatty 48
    finding 83
    keeping it fresh 92
    safe 7, 83, 84
    survival biscuits 98–9
    taste of cooked animals 96
    wild foods 84–9
freezer bags, resealable 130
freezing to death 45, 46–7
friends, sticking with 6
frostbite 46
fruit acids 94, 99

gaffer tape (duct tape) 128
gangrene 46
garlic mustard 87
Genghis Khan 92
Gobi Desert, Central Asia 65
golden rules of survival 6–7
gooseberries 87
goosebumps 39, 45
GPS (Global Positioning System) 24–5
grass blanket 54
Greeks, ancient 17
green bamboo 62
Greenwich, London 23

hats 5, 6, 39, 41, 44
heart rate 4

heatstroke 40, 41, 42
herbs 130
horse manure 54
hyperthermia 40
hypothermia 40

Inuits 48

jungle 62–3

kindling 51, 52, 95
kufiyya 43

landscapes, noting 11
latitude 22, 23
leadership 112–13
LEDs (light emitting diodes) 128
let someone know where you're going 10, 33, 35
Little Dipper 17
long Johns 48
longitude 22–3

magnetic field 15
magnetic north/south poles 15
magnifying glass 126
malnutrition 77
maps 19, 20–21, 32, 115, 126
Mars, living on 39
Milky Way Galaxy 16–17
mirror 111, 127, 129
Moon, living on the 39
Morse, Samuel Finley Breese 111
Morse code 109–11, 116
mountain rescue 118
mulberries 88

navigation
    desert 16
    following a heading 21–2
    Viking 28
nettles 88
night sky 16, 17
Nobile, Umberto 56–7, 58–9
Norsemen 28
North Pole 15, 17, 22, 56, 57
North Star (Pole Star) 16, 17, 18

oven, pizza box 100–101

pasta 92
pencil and paper 126
penguins 28
pine resin 50
planets 17
plastic sheet, large 129
polar bears 28, 64
prime meridian 22–3
protein 83, 90, 97
pulsars 109

quiz, survival 132–5

radio 58, 103, 116, 117
rain water 69, 76–7, 129
raspberries 88
red skies 27
rescuers 6, 7
rice 92

Sahara Desert 65
SAS 47
satellites 24, 25

Scott, Captain Robert 56, 126
SET (Search for Extraterrestrial
    Intelligence) 109
shelter
    adapted 54
    desert 55
    leaf and branch 54
    making a 7, 39, 52, 103,
        129
    natural 54
    shop-bought 55
    types of 53–5
shepherd's purse 89
shivering 39, 45
shoes 5, 47, 129
sign: visible to rescuers 7, 58
Sinai Desert 65
sleds 49
slit trench 54
smoke signals 108–9
solar oven 100–101
solar still 70–71
SOS messages 109, 110, 111,
    116
south, finding the (using stars) 18
South Pole 15, 22, 56, 126
Southern Cross 18
spices 130
stars
    desert navigation by 16
    pulsating 109
    use to find the south 18
staying put 12
storm shell 48, 49
strawberries 89
sun block 67, 129
sun compass 28, 29

sunscreen 39
survival quiz 132–5
survival stories
    cannibalism 102–5
    stranded on the ice 56–9
    survival in an open boat 75–9
    trapped on a fishing trip 33–5
sweating 39, 40, 41, 49, 67,
    129
sweets, boiled 131
swimming 4

temperature
    cold 45–9
    hot 40–44, 65
    ideal 39, 47
    reducing 42
tents 55, 57–8, 69
tepee fire 51
thermometer 38
tinder 50, 51, 52, 126
Tour de France 83
tracks
    animal 114
    tracking signs 119–21
treasure map 32, 115

urine 68–9, 71

Vail, Alfred 111
Viking navigation 28

wandering about 6
'wandering stars' 17
water
    bees and 66
    birds and 63

water cont.
    in the human body 66
    salt 78, 79
    as a sun block 67
water, drinking
    amount needed each day 68
    avoiding heatstroke 41
    boiling 64, 73, 74
    drinking too much 69
    importance of 7, 66–7, 84
    rain water 69, 76–7, 129
    solar still 70–71
    water filter 72–4
    the 'wee' test 68–9
water sources
    Arctic and Antarctic 64
    desert 65
    jungle 62–3
    mountain 63
weather prediction 27, 33
Webster, Dr Ellis 33–5
Western Desert 65
wet wipes 130
whistle 118, 127
wild leek 89
wildlife 5, 83
wind
    desert 43
    speeds 26
worms 97, 130
wristwatch, compass 30–31

Also available from
Macmillan Children's Books
in association with the science of...

YOUR PLANET NEEDS YOU!
A Kids' Guide to Going Green
Dave Reay
978-0-330-45095-9
£4.99

Maximus, Saviour of Worlds, Protector of Humankind and Chocolate Fanatic, has been given a mission: stop the planet from heating up, and do it fast!

Join Max and his sidekicks Henry and Flora as they become global warming warriors, taking on the big climate culprits one by one. They'll give you some top tips about energy conservation at home, in the classroom, in the garden . . . from recycling to compost to turning off that switch!

OUCH!
Extreme Feats of Human Endurance
Georgina Phillips
978-0-330-45405-6
£3.99

Did you hear about the brave mountain climber who sliced off his own hand? Or Ernest Shackleton, who set off across the Antarctic Continent facing frostbite, storms and sub-zero waters? Or the man who had to put up with a nasty case of the hiccups – for a horrifying 68 years!

This mind-boggling book is packed with bizarre survival stories that prove just how amazing the human mind and body can be.

All Pan Macmillan titles can be ordered from our website, www.panmacmillan.com, or from your local bookshop and are also available by post from:

Bookpost, PO Box 29, Douglas, Isle of Man IM99 1BQ

Credit cards accepted. For details:
Telephone: 01624 677267
Fax: 01624 670923
Email: bookshop@enterprise.net
www.bookpost.co.uk

Free postage and packing in the United Kindgom